Cases in Portfolio Management

John W. Peavy III, CFA
Katrina F. Sherrerd, CFA

Additional copies of this publication may be ordered from:

Association for Investment Management and Research
P.O. Box 7947
Charlottesville, VA 22906
Telephone: 804/980-3647
Fax: 804/977-0350

The Association for Investment Management and Research
comprises the Institute of Chartered Financial Analysts
and the Financial Analysts Federation.

Charlene E. Semer, *Associate Editor*
Jaynee M. Dudley, *Assistant Editor*
Nina D. Hutchinson, *Typesetting/Layout*

ISBN 1-879087-04-9

Printed in the United States of America

Table of Contents

List of cases   v

Preface   vii

Introduction   1

Cases   9

Guideline answers   51

Appendix   107

List of Cases

	Cases	*Guideline Answers*
Individual Investors		
The Mason Family (A)	11	53
The Mason Family (B)	14	56
The Allen Family (A)	15	58
The Allen Family (B)	18	62
The Ramez Family (A)	19	64
The Ramez Family (B)	22	67
Institutional Investors		
Ednam Products Company	23	69
Mid-South Trucking Company	26	75
General Technology Corporation (A)	29	77
General Technology Corporation (B)	32	80
Profit-Sharing Advisory, Inc. (A)	33	81
Profit-Sharing Advisory, Inc. (B)	35	83
Industrial Products Corporation (A)	36	85
Industrial Products Corporation (B)	37	87
Industrial Products Corporation (C)	38	88
Universal Products, Inc.	39	90
World Ecosystem Consortium (A)	42	96
World Ecosystem Consortium (B)	44	99
Good Samaritan Hospital (A)	45	101
Good Samaritan Hospital (B)	49	103
Good Samaritan Hospital (C)	50	106

Preface

The Chartered Financial Analyst examination program recognizes the importance of the portfolio management process. As a CFA candidate, you are exposed to an extensive set of readings on ethics and professional standards, accounting, economics, quantitative analysis, equity analysis, fixed-income analysis, and portfolio management. The study of these disciplines provides the tools an investment manager needs to construct optimal portfolios. Knowledge about each of these separate disciplines is not sufficient, however; without the ability to apply them, the investment manager cannot succeed.

In the Level I and Level II examinations, you are exposed to the tools of portfolio management. A substantial portion of the Level III examination focuses on their application in the portfolio management process. Now comes the challenging and rewarding task of applying this abundance of knowledge and information. Portfolio management is where the action is: moving step-by-step through the orderly process of converting raw inputs into a portfolio that maximizes expected return relative to the investor's ability to bear risk, given the investor's constraints and preferences, the expectational factors, and market uncertainties.

The intent of this portfolio management casebook is to provide practical applications of the techniques, concepts, and theories presented throughout the CFA study program. The cases challenge you to combine your skills and tools with judgment and creativity to solve realistic problems. The value of the case method comes from the process of distilling facts and circumstances and determining an appropriate course of action based on available information.

The case method is a self-study approach. Unlike the CFA examination, no specific questions are to be answered. In fact, no particular answer is the only and irrefutable one. Instead, you apply your knowledge and experience to the specific situation and determine an appropriate investment policy and asset allocation. In each case, at a minimum, you should accomplish the following:

1. Identify the problem. Determine what action(s) is(are) necessary to respond properly to the case situation.

2. Prepare an investment policy statement that accurately specifies the investor's objectives, constraints, and preferences or unique circumstances.

3. Prepare a recommended asset allocation that reflects the investment policy and relevant economic, political, and financial market considerations.

4. Provide a framework for monitoring investor-related input factors and economic and market input factors so that the portfolio can be adjusted appropriately and as necessary.

In all cases, you should justify the actions you recommend.

We encourage you to analyze each case carefully and completely. Use the concepts outlined in the Introduction as a framework. Prepare a response to the case situation before consulting any reference source. In this manner, you can better determine your grasp of the tools and knowledge as they apply in a real-time setting. Model answers are provided so that you can compare your response to an "idealized" representative answer. These guideline answers are more comprehensive than would be the responses under actual CFA examination conditions, in which time constraints preclude this amount of detail. We believe, however, that your review of and reflection on these guideline answers will enhance your ability to analyze and effectively respond to the portfolio management situations you will encounter in practice.

We are particularly grateful to James R. Vertin, CFA, for his extensive and generous contribution of time and creative suggestions to the development and production of this casebook. Additional thanks are due to Gordon T. Wise, CFA, and Fred H. Speece, CFA, both members of the Institute of Chartered Financial Analysts' Candidate Curriculum Committee, for helping in the development of the cases. We also appreciate the constructive support of Darwin M. Bayston, CFA, Thomas A. Bowman, CFA, and Robert M. Luck, CFA.

John W. Peavy III, CFA
Katrina F. Sherrerd, CFA
November 1990

Introduction

Since the seminal work of Harry Markowitz in the 1950s, which led to the development of modern portfolio theory, the investment management profession has continued to evolve. Markowitz held that an investment manager should evaluate the interrelationship among assets as opposed to analyzing each asset in isolation. His approach, emphasizing the collective importance of all an investor's holdings, set the cornerstone for the portfolio management process. Markowitz's identification of the risk-return trade-off in a portfolio context has found widespread acceptance and application among investment managers.

In recent years, managers have broadened their perspectives from individual asset selection to portfolio balance. This approach emphasizes diversification and the contribution of asset characteristics to a portfolio that will best achieve the financial objectives of each investor, within the personal, economic, and financial constraints that prevail at the time. This casebook is a practicum on how to apply that approach. Although the cases are hypothetical, the situations they present are quite practical. Working through these cases is an opportunity to put the portfolio management process into practice, to compare your strategy recommendations with those reached by others, and to analyze different ways to achieve a given end.

The remainder of this introduction sets up the framework for your consideration of the situations posed in the cases. It draws upon, but does not supplant, the readings recommended for CFA candidates, particularly *Managing Investment Portfolios*.[1] You will probably want to refer back to the full text of some of these readings as you develop your response to the cases. The introduction also lays out the definitional conventions upon which the guideline answers are based.

The Portfolio Management Process

The portfolio management process consists of an integrated, consistent set of steps by which an investment manager creates and maintains appropriate combinations of investment assets. As depicted in Figure 1, it is a dynamic and flexible process, complete with feedback loops, monitoring, and adjustment. This process generally comprises the following steps:

1.   Identification and evaluation of the investor's objectives, preferences, and constraints as a basis for developing an investment policy specific to that investor;

---

[1]John L. Maginn, CFA, and Donald L. Tuttle, CFA, eds., *Managing Investment Portfolios*, second edition, Charlottesville: Association for Investment Management and Research, 1990.

2. Formulation of appropriate investment strategies and their implementation through selection of optimal combinations of financial and real assets in the marketplace;

3. Monitoring of market conditions, relative asset values, and the investor's circumstances; and

4. Adjustment of the portfolio as is appropriate to reflect significant change in any of the relevant variables.

The mechanics of the process vary from manager to manager. Each manager has a preferred *modus operandi* that is uniquely his or her own, which is as it should be. The process itself, however, is common to all managers everywhere.

Figure 1.

The Portfolio Construction, Monitoring, and Revision Process

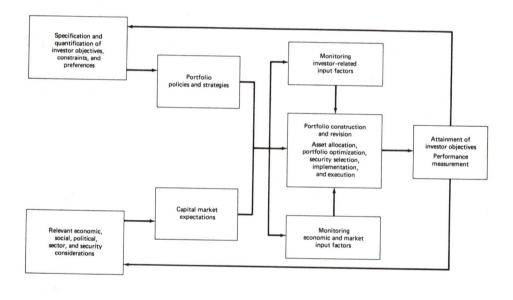

Source: Managing Investment Portfolios, 1990.

Fiduciary Responsibilities

The investment management process is bounded by judicial standards developed through common law and by laws and regulations enforced by a number of federal and state agencies. On the federal level, these bodies include the Securities and Exchange Commission, the Internal Revenue Service, and the Department of Labor. Because state laws governing trust management have evolved largely through the courts, and are still evolving, laws and institutional oversight arrangements vary widely from state to state. Investment managers should thoroughly understand the current legal constraints of the states in which they operate.

One of the most elusive concepts governing fiduciaries is the Prudent Man rule.[2] This rule is in virtually all instances the court-accepted standard for management of individual trust funds. State courts have extended the concept, with some variations, to the management of investments for endowment funds of nonprofit organizations, and federal law has adapted the Prudent Man standard to the investment of employee benefit (retirement) funds.

The Prudent Man appeared on the American scene in 1830, but it was not stated formally until the 1940s. A model statute, developed by the American Bankers Association for state adoption, includes the following language:

> . . . a fiduciary shall exercise the judgment and care, under the circumstances then prevailing, which men of prudence, discretion and intelligence exercise in the management of their own affairs . . .

Almost all present-day statutory standards are variations on this model.

The main virtue of the Prudent Man rule, in theory, is its flexibility. Unlike a specific list of investment "dos" and "don'ts," interpretation of the Prudent Man standard can bend and evolve with the times and circumstances. In many cases, however, judicial rulings have rigidly defined what types of investments are and are not considered prudent. Further, in state law governing private trusts, the Prudent Man standard continues to be applied to individual investments rather than to the composition of a whole portfolio, an interpretation some observers characterize as rigid and anachronistic.

Since 1974, the U.S. Labor Department has administered the Employment Retirement Income Security Act (ERISA), which regulates employer-sponsored retirement plans. ERISA essentially has four standards governing the management of pension funds: prudence, loyalty, reasonable administrative cost, and diversification. The duty of prudence requires that fiduciaries perform their duties

> . . . with the care, skill, prudence and diligence under the circumstances then prevailing that a prudent man acting in a like capacity and familiar with such matters would use in the conduct of an enterprise of a like character and with like aims.

The term "familiar with such matters" has been interpreted as a "Prudent Expert" rule, according to which a manager must meet the standard for a trained, experienced investment professional rather than merely that of a "prudent man." The duty of loyalty requires that a fiduciary use plan assets only to provide benefits for participants and beneficiaries and to defray *reasonable* administrative expenses. The diversification rule requires that fiduciaries diversify plan investments so as to minimize the risk of large losses, unless doing so under the circumstances at hand clearly would not be prudent. The circumstances to be considered include the

---

[2]For a thorough discussion of the Prudent Man standard, see Beth Longstreth, "The Prudent Man Rule Today—Variations on a Single Theme," in 1991 CFA Candidate Readings—Level II, Charlottesville: The Institute of Chartered Financial Analysts,1990, pp. 10-40.

purposes of the plan, the amount of plan assets, financial and industrial conditions, the type of investment, geographical distribution, and maturity dates. A significant evolutionary aspect of ERISA's standards is that they apply not to an individual portfolio investment but *to management of the portfolio as a whole.*

Individual Investors

The first three sets of cases in this casebook—those concerning the Mason, the Allen, and the Ramez families—address the management of portfolios for individual investors, a challenging and dynamic process. The characteristics of individual investors and the circumstances and opportunities that confront them are more diverse and complex than for any other class of investor.

Each individual's financial profile is unique. Each has a different liquidity need, time horizon, and set of constraints. Many have a combination of taxable and nontaxable portfolios. Many do not have a full grasp of either their own risk tolerance or the risk characteristics of the wide array of assets available to them. Psychological characteristics also play an important role in managing investments for individuals.

A carefully planned investment policy for an individual investor must incorporate all of the unique factors pertaining to that investor. Investment objectives must be defined in terms of return requirements and risk tolerance. Constraints, such as liquidity, time horizon, taxes, and legal or regulatory matters, must be recognized explicitly and allowed for in order to achieve the investor's objectives. Preferences, which are self-imposed constraints, must be identified and respected.

The investment policy for each investor is embodied in an operational statement that sets forth guidelines specifying the actions to be taken to achieve the investor's financial objectives within the constraints imposed and the preferences desired. Many portfolio investment considerations are qualitative, but all lead to quantification of return and risk requirements that can be translated into an efficient, individually tailored portfolio.

Individuals Contrasted With Institutions

The Good Samaritan Hospital cases in this book point up some of the differences in individual and institutional portfolio management. One observer has identified these differences as follows:

- Individuals define risk as "losing money" or "doing something that feels uncomfortable," while institutions use quantitative concepts, such as standard deviation of returns, to define risk.
- Individuals can be categorized by their personalities or "psychographics," while institutions can be categorized by the investment characteristics of those who have a beneficial interest in their portfolios.
- Individuals can be defined financially by their assets and goals, while institutions are generally a more precise package of assets and liabilities or endowment funding requirements.

- Individuals are free to act as they see fit, while institutions are subject to legal and regulatory constraints.
- Most individuals have to contend with the added complexity of taxes, while many institutions are free of such considerations under normal circumstances.[3]

Important additional differences are in time horizon and in life-cycle changes. The assumption of infinite life used in planning many institutional portfolios has no parallel in individual investment planning. Also, individuals experience an economic shift between youth and old age, while institutions maintain a relatively constant economic profile over time.

Institutional Investors

Institutional investors encompass a variety of nonprofit and for-profit entities, such as pension plans, endowment funds, insurance companies, banks, and mutual funds, among which investment policy considerations vary widely. Management of institutional portfolios has become increasingly complex and challenging. Modern portfolio theory, rapidly changing capital markets, performance pressures, and an increasing array of new financial instruments challenge even the most competent investment manager. The complexity of portfolio management increases the importance of establishing a well-defined and effective investment policy that clearly defines objectives, risk tolerance, and investment constraints and preferences.

Charles Ellis states that an investment policy should establish guidelines that are genuinely appropriate to the realities of the investor's objectives and the realities of the investment marketplace.[4] The principal reason for emphasizing establishment of *long-term* investment policy is to prevent arbitrary or impulsive revisions of a sound basic policy design and to help the portfolio manager continue to plan and execute in a *long-term* context at times when short-term pressures might otherwise cause the manager to abandon it.

In articulating an investment policy, the prudent portfolio manager would be well advised to respond to the following questions posed by Ellis, which apply with equal appropriateness to individual investors:

- Is the policy carefully designed to meet the real needs and objectives of the client?
- Is the policy written clearly enough so that a competent stranger could manage the portfolio and satisfy the client's needs?
- Would the client have been able to sustain commitment to the policy during the capital markets that have actually been experienced over past years?

---

[3]Ronald W. Kaiser, "Institutional Investors," in *Managing Investment Portfolios,* second edition, Charlottesville: Association for Investment Management and Research, 1990, p. 3-2.

[4]Charles D. Ellis, *Investment Policy, How to Win the Loser's Game,* Homewood, Illinois: Business One Irwin, 1985.

- Would the investment manager have been able to maintain fidelity to the policy during the same periods?
- Would the policy have achieved the client's objectives?

The key factors that affect the investment behavior of an institution may differ considerably from the factors that influence most individual investors. Among these important factors are the nature of the institution's obligations to its clients, its tax status, and the legal and regulatory requirements that govern its operation. The institution's investment manager must understand these factors and also have a good grasp of such intangible considerations as the institution's goals and psychology. Each of these elements must be weighed in determining an optimal investment policy for the institution.

As is the case with individual investors, an institutional investment policy must account for all the unique factors pertaining to that investor. Return requirements and risk tolerance must be specifically stated to define an appropriate investment objective. The manager must adhere to investment constraints and preferences and recognize prospective as well as current capital market considerations in attempting to achieve the identified investment objectives.

Retirement Plans

The investing of pension funds may be taken as illustrative of institutional investment in general. Pension plans accumulate capital to meet future benefit payments and, in the process, have become the largest holders of institutional capital.

Retirement plans are of two basic forms: defined-benefit plans and defined-contribution plans. Although both plans have the common objective of accumulating capital to meet future benefit payments, the differences between them require significantly different investment policies. The Ednam Products Company case illustrates an approach used with a defined-contribution plan in which employess control their own investments. Several of the other institutional investor cases in the book deal with defined-benefit plans.

The objectives of pension plans are a complex combination of the objectives of the plan sponsor, of the pension plan itself, and of its beneficiaries. Each plan must develop a portfolio policy that properly reflects its unique objectives, risk tolerance, constraints, and preferences. The most important considerations are the need to fund the plan and to avoid significant losses. The failure of a pension fund to achieve satisfactory performance may reflect the absence of a clear, concise statement of investment policy.

Endowment Funds

A broad range of nonprofit institutions, including religious organizations, educational institutions, cultural entities, private social agencies, hospitals, trade associations, and corporate and private foundations, depend on endowment funds. Although often compared with retirement funds in terms of investment objectives and constraints, endowment funds in fact share only two major similarities: they are both usually long-term in nature, and with minor exceptions, they are not taxable.

The range of objectives of endowment funds is extremely broad, and definitions of these objectives are often highly qualitative in nature. In this sense, they resemble individual investors. The determination of the investment policy for an endowment fund is the resolution of a creative tension existing between the highly demanding immediate needs for income to meet the present objectives of the institution and the pervasive and enduring pressures for an inflation-protected, growing stream of income to meet tomorrow's demands. These considerations are a factor in the Good Samaritan Hospital set of cases, which deals with investment policy for an endowed institution.

The Case Approach

The literature about portfolio management has proliferated in recent years. No amount of reading about the portfolio management process, however, substitutes adequately for the actual practice of the process. In this casebook, we provide a diverse array of portfolio management cases that allow you to apply your management knowledge and experience to real-life investment situations. With each case, we challenge you to identify and specify the investor's objectives, preferences, and constraints and to develop appropriate investment policies and strategies. Next, you must select an optimal combination of investment assets subject to specific capital market and individual asset characteristics and expectations. You complete the portfolio management cycle by monitoring market conditions, relative asset values, and investor circumstances, and adjusting the portfolio as necessary through time.

The investment manager must be able to use the portfolio management process effectively regardless of type of client or the client's investment philosophy, preferences, or approach. This casebook offers exposure to the application of the portfolio management process across a variety of customers with many different investment objectives, constraints, and preferences. Some of the cases will challenge your ability to evaluate international and real estate assets, in addition to the traditional domestic financial assets.

Guideline answers follow the case studies. Each answer is an example of an *appropriate* solution to the case; it is not necessarily the one *right* solution. In the interest of uniformity, the guideline answers incorporate certain conventions. Federal, state, and local income taxes, for example, are assumed always to total 40 percent. The historical data used as benchmark returns and levels of risk throughout the guideline answers are shown on the next page. These compound annual rates of return and standard deviations for broad asset classes are for the 30-year period, 1960 through 1989 (except as noted).

Table A in the appendix provides similar data in greater detail. To illustrate the effect of portfolio longevity on rate of return, Table A also shows compound annual rates of return for 5-, 10-, and 20-year holding periods. Appendix Table B presents a correlation matrix for returns in major asset classes for the 1971-87 period. The correlations measure the degree to which returns on any two assets move in unison and the sensitivity of the returns to inflation.

Asset Class	Annual Rate of Return	Standard Deviation
Domestic (U.S.) equities	10.29	15.89
International equities*	12.46	22.50
Corporate bonds	6.88	11.29
Municipal bonds	6.37	2.44
Long-term Treasury bonds	6.42	11.06
Treasury bills	6.34	2.90
Real estate**	12.24	4.91
Real GNP growth	3.14	
Inflation rate (CPI)	4.97	

---

*   1969-89.

**   1978-89. Because real estate data are based on appraisals rather than sales price, returns are not completely comparable to those of other assets and the standard deviation is artificially low.

In most of the guideline answers, "generic" rather than specific asset classes are used in the suggested portfolios—"cash equivalents," for example, rather than Treasury bills, money market funds, or other highly liquid forms. Where historical data are given for these "generic" assets, they are represented by the following series from Appendix Table A:

Cash equivalents — Treasury bills
Domestic stocks — Common stocks
International stocks — EAFE Index
Domestic bonds — Corporate bonds
Equity real estate — Commercial property index
Tax-exempt bonds — Municipal bonds

Now, on to the cases! We hope you will find them intriguing, challenging, and instructive.

Cases

The Mason Family (A)

Paul Water, CFA, is a managing partner of SPW, Inc., an investment counseling firm specializing in domestic stocks and bonds. Water takes pride in his ability to establish and carry out investment policies that are tailored to the specific circumstances and needs of individuals and families. Currently, he is reviewing his notes on the Mason family account.

The Masons
Dr. Perrie Mason is an electrical engineer, inventor, and long-time professor at the Essex Institute. After 30 years of teaching, she learned that the rights to one of her patented inventions, the "inverse return valve," were acquired by a new electronics company, ACS, Inc. In anticipation of such an event, Dr. Mason had established a private corporation, wholly owned by the Mason family, to hold the valve patent. ACS is acquiring this corporation from the Masons for $1 million in cash, payable at the closing in 30 days. ACS has also agreed to pay continuing royalties to Dr. Mason or her heirs, based on its sales of systems that use the valve.

Because ACS has no operating record as yet, neither the company nor Dr. Mason has a historical basis for forecasting future sales and royalties. Although all parties are optimistic about prospects for success, they also are aware of the risks associated with any new firm, especially one exposed to the technological obsolescence that is characteristic of the electronics industry. ACS management has informed Dr. Mason that she might expect royalties up to $100,000 in the first year of production and maximum royalties up to $500,000 annually thereafter for an indefinite period.

Investment Considerations
Water is particularly interested in the Masons' income requirements. Dr. Mason, who is 60 years old, earns $50,000 annually at the Essex Institute. Mr. Mason, who is 70 years old, retired from his own career 12 years ago to help Dr. Mason with her research efforts. A small income from irregular speaking engagements supplements his annual retirement income of $25,000. Their combined annual income averages $80,000. Aside from a modest equity in their home, the Masons have no financial assets; their savings have been invested in Dr. Mason's inventions. Dr. Mason plans to retire from Essex at the end of the year to devote her time to travel, charity, and special research projects. All of the Masons' three children are married and have families of their own.

The Masons desire to help with the education of their grandchildren and have included specific provisions to this effect in their wills. In addition, Mr. Mason wants to establish a scholarship fund at Essex in his wife's name. He has not decided whether to make annual contributions or to leave a bequest in his will to fund this scholarship.

The Task

The Masons are eager to know how their money will be invested, given their priorities. Water reviewed his notes one more time to make sure that he had all of the facts. He identified two specific tasks to be completed prior to his upcoming meeting with the Masons:

- Develop an investment policy for the Masons' $1 million portfolio; and
- Determine an asset allocation that reflects the investment objectives, constraints, and preferences detailed in the investment policy.

Water also reviewed his firm's economic forecast (see Exhibit 1), current capital market conditions (Exhibit 2), and the firm's capital market outlook for the next 12 months (Exhibit 3). SPW is forecasting a high probability of either stagflation or disinflation. Water also noted that the firm is forecasting long-run annual returns on common stocks of 8 percent and on bonds of 6 percent. He will incorporate these capital market expectations into his asset allocation recommendation.

Exhibit 1

SPW's Economic Forecast

SPW anticipates three possible economic scenarios during the next 12 months: stagflation, disinflation, or accelerating inflation. These scenarios are summarized as follows:

Scenario	Nominal GNP	GNP Deflator
Stagflation (45% probability)	9.7%	7.5%
Disinflation (35% probability)	6.6	5.0
Inflation (20% probability)	15.4	10.0

These numbers are based on the following conditions:

Stagflation: Continuing budget deficits, a Federal Reserve policy that is accommodative of large government credit demands, higher levels of nominal interest rates, some "crowding out" of private investment spending, and somewhat slower economic growth.

Disinflation/Slow Growth: Slower growth in the money supply, resulting in lower inflation and, eventually, lower nominal interest rates; high federal government deficits and slower rates of economic growth, which reduce private investment spending.

Accelerating Inflation/Rapid Growth: Inflation accelerating to double digits, and real GNP growth at above-average rates; a Federal Reserve policy that accommodates large federal budget deficits; higher levels of spending, which increase employment and national income; rising nominal interest rates and an overheated economy.

Exhibit 2
Current Capital Market Conditions

	Current Yield Levels	*Historical Standard Deviation of Total Returns*
Cash equivalents	9.0%	2.8%
Domestic bonds	12.0	2.6
Domestic stocks	4.0	15.6

Exhibit 3
Twelve-Month Capital Market Outlook

	*Total Expected Annual Return**	*Expected Annual Yield*
Stagflation		
(45% probability)		
Cash equivalents	9.5%	10.0%
Domestic bonds	3.4	13.0
Domestic stocks	2.2	4.5
Disinflation		
(35% probability)		
Cash equivalents	8.4%	6.0%
Domestic bonds	34.0	10.0
Domestic stocks	24.9	3.0
Inflation		
(20% probability)		
Cash equivalents	11.0%	16.0%
Domestic bonds	−10.3	15.0
Domestic stocks	19.4	6.0

* The assumed annual dividend growth rates for common stocks are 10% in stagflation, 7% in disinflation, and 14% in inflation.

The Mason Family (B)

Several years later, Mr. Mason whose own health is deteriorating, telephoned Water to inform him that Dr. Mason had died. Water immediately requested a meeting with Mr. Mason to discuss the investment policy in light of these changes.

In the meeting, Mason indicates that he has decided to use his royalty income to set up a scholarship fund in the name of his wife for the benefit of enterprising young engineers attending the Essex Institute and that he still wants to assist financially in the education of his grandchildren. He plans to leave all of his assets to his children and grandchildren, with a special bequest to the Essex Institute.

Water confirms that after all estate taxes are paid, the value of the Mason portfolio will be $2.5 million. The royalties from Dr. Mason's invention are expected to average $200,000 a year indefinitely.

Water ponders the change in circumstances. He wants to make sure that the revised investment policy statement will adequately consider Mr. Mason's uncertain health and his priorities. Then, Water will reevaluate the asset allocation. The portfolio is currently invested in "blue chip" stocks (70 percent) and high-grade bonds (30 percent).

Water notes that, coincidentally, his firm's current capital market expectations are the same today as they were when he first met the Masons.

The Allen Family (A)

Harvey Bowles, CFA, recently joined Perennial Trust Company, a firm specializing in financial management for wealthy families. Bowles' first assignment is the Allen family, a new client who came to Perennial upon the death of Charles A. Allen. Bowles soon will be meeting with Mr. Allen's widow, Emily Allen, and son, George Allen. To familiarize himself with the Allens' situation, he reads the following memorandum prepared by Perennial's new-business officer:

Emily Allen is the Allen trust's only income beneficiary. Upon her death, the assets go to her son, George, free of taxes (which were paid at Mr. Allen's death). Emily Allen is 65 years old and is suffering from a physically degenerative disease; although her mind is quite alert, she is not expected to live more than a few more years. Mrs. Allen has good insurance, but it does not cover all of her growing medical bills. Beyond her substantial medical bills, Mrs. Allen has few expenses. She contributes most of her excess income to various charities and occasionally makes gifts to George and members of his family. She feels that George is somewhat irresponsible but is a good son, husband, and father. Mrs. Allen lived through the Depression and is concerned about the present-day financial environment. She has often said, "We saw great companies and great fortunes destroyed. We were terrified, and we suffered great hardship; yet, my husband was able to build our fortune by investing wisely over the years." The Allen trust's only investment restriction is a requirement that George Allen be consulted, as a courtesy, before any investment action is taken.

George Allen, 44, is married and has three sons (two in prep school and one in college). Although Mr. Allen is not employed, he volunteers his services to a variety of civic and charitable organizations. Neither he nor his wife, a homemaker, seems to be financially sophisticated, although Mr. Allen is a strong believer in free investment markets and free enterprise. He believes that "smart investors can double their money every five years." He looks forward to financing businesses for his sons as they graduate from college. The George Allens' living style and family needs require an annual after-tax income of $100,000. This now is derived from investment income and occasional gifts from his mother. He wants to increase the income from his portfolio to eliminate his dependence on gifts from his mother.

The present status of the Allen trust is shown in Exhibit 1, and George Allen's current investment portfolio is shown in Exhibit 2. The real estate investment in that portfolio is a piece of the real estate investment owned in the trust.

Exhibit 1

Investment Assets: Charles A. Allen Trust

	Cost	Market Value	After-Tax Yield
Cash equivalents	$ 3,000,000	$ 3,000,000	4%
Growth stocks	500,000	1,000,000	1
Cyclical stocks	1,000,000	1,000,000	2
Defensive stocks	3,000,000	4,000,000	2
Tax-exempt bonds	4,000,000	4,500,000	7
Equity real estate*	1,000,000	2,000,000	6
Total	$12,500,000	$15,500,000	

* Exclusive of personal residence.

Exhibit 2

Investment Assets: George Allen

	Cost	Market Value	After-Tax Yield
Money market account	$ 50,000	$ 50,000	3%
Growth stocks	150,000	300,000	1
Cyclical stocks	200,000	250,000	2
Defensive stocks	300,000	400,000	2
Venture capital fund	100,000	100,000	0
Tax-exempt bonds	300,000	400,000	7
Equity real estate*	200,000	300,000	6
Total	$1,300,000	$1,800,000	

* Exclusive of personal residence.

Before his meeting with the Allens, Bowles reviews Perennial's latest investment return projections. His firm believes that continued prosperity is the most likely outlook for the next three to five years but is mindful of the possibility of two disturbing alternatives: a return to high inflation, or a drift into deflation/depression. Exhibit 3 presents the details of Perennial's projections.

Bowles lists the tasks to be completed prior to his upcoming meeting. The first is to create revised investment policy statements for the Allen trust and for George Allen. The second is to recommend a new asset allocation for each Allen portfolio.

He realizes that he must justify any changes he recommends and explain why they are appropriate.

Exhibit 3

Perennial Trust Company
Three- to Five-Year Expected Annual Investment Returns

	Expected Total Annual Return	Expected Annual Yield
Continued prosperity **(60% probability)**		
Cash equivalents	5%	5%
Domestic stocks	14	4
Domestic bonds	13	13
Tax-exempt bonds	7	7
Equity real estate	9	10
High inflation **(20% probability)**		
Cash equivalents	9%	9%
Domestic stocks	16	5
Domestic bonds	6	16
Tax-exempt bonds	2	8
Equity real estate	14	10
Deflation/depression **(20% probability)**		
Cash equivalents	2%	2%
Domestic stocks	−5	2.
Domestic bonds	25	9
Tax-exempt bonds	15	5
Equity real estate	−3	5

The Allen Family (B)

Nine months later, Emily Allen requested a meeting with Bowles to discuss her portfolio. After this meeting, Bowles knows that he must review the Allen trust's policy and investment mix. He rereads the memorandum summarizing his meeting with Emily.

> Mrs. Allen announced that her disease has been arrested. The Lifeline Company discovered a new drug that successfully counteracts the virus that had been attacking her. This "miracle drug," as she calls it, has changed her perspective on life. She now looks forward to exploring the world and seeing the sights she had thought she would never be able to see. She also wants to make a substantial donation to medical research in the name of her late husband, Charles. Because she does not control the assets of the trust and is entitled only to its annual income, Mrs. Allen reasons that she would have to make gifts of $250,000 a year for 10 years to meet her goal. Mrs. Allen does not plan to provide any further support to her son; in fact, she would prefer that he get a job. She is willing to help with the education of the grandchildren.

Bowles prepares to revise his previous investment policy statements and asset allocations for each of the Allen portfolios. Although he looks forward to revising the Allen trust portfolio, he is not looking forward to his "consult" meeting with George Allen, who had insisted at their previous meeting that his portfolio be managed to generate annual income of at least $100,000 after taxes.

The Ramez Family (A)

Martina Lindell, CFA, is reviewing the file of the Ramez family, her first non-U.S. client. This client is especially important to her firm, Dexter Associates, because it is beginning to expand its services internationally. Lindell is to provide recommendations on asset allocation for the Ramez portfolio and on whether the firm should engage an outside manager for the international equities to be included.

Dexter Associates

Dexter's management process is "top-down." The firm begins with broadly defined economic scenarios and proceeds in a systematic, disciplined manner to asset allocation and security selection. For many years, the firm has included only domestic stocks and bonds in its portfolios. This year, however, it has decided to broaden the asset classes available for client portfolios by adding equity real estate, international equities, and precious metals. The firm has proceeded cautiously in this and has not yet brought into the firm all the personnel required to manage the three new asset classes.

Dexter Associates prides itself on its economic forecasts. Exhibit 1 contains the current three- to five-year forecast of expected annual total return, yield, and standard deviation under three possible economic scenarios. The firm believes that the most likely scenario is one of low growth and low inflation.

The Ramez Family

Luis and Inez Ramez have recently sold their family business for $10 million and immigrated to the United States from the Philippines. They have been accepted for residence in the United States and intend to become U.S. citizens. After a few years of travel and leisure, Luis intends to return to business. He plans to use a portion of the proceeds from the sale of his business to fund a new business venture. Inez expects to pursue charitable activities benefiting needy Philippine families throughout the world.

The Ramezes have three children. Pedro, 19, is a student in Paris who intends to practice medicine in his native Philippines. Marco, 23, lives with his wife in Singapore, where they have recently begun an international import/export company. Maria, 25, lives in Panama with her husband, a banker, and their two children. She is currently enrolled in a masters program in political science. Although Luis and Inez have carefully raised their children to be self-reliant and self-supporting, they intend to pay for their children's and grandchildren's education and occasionally to provide for special needs the children encounter. The children are not aware of the

Exhibit 1

**Capital Market Outlook
Three- to Five-Year Projections**

	Expected Annual Total Return	Expected Annual Yield	Expected Annual Standard Deviation
Low growth, low inflation (60% probability)			
Cash equivalents	5%	5%	3%
Domestic bonds	11	8	15
Domestic stocks	15	3	22
International stocks	11	2	25
Equity real estate	8	7	2
Precious metals	0	0	12
Rapid growth, high inflation (20% probability)			
Cash equivalents	10%	10%	3%
Domestic bonds	−12	12	17
Domestic stocks	8	4	20
International stocks	16	3	22
Equity real estate	14	7	7
Precious metals	20	0	15
Depression/deflation (20% probability)			
Cash equivalents	2%	2%	3%
Domestic bonds	15	6	13
Domestic stocks	−12	1	24
International stocks	−14	1.5	27
Equity real estate	0	0	7
Precious metals	5	0	12

extent of the family wealth.

The proceeds of the sale of the Philippines business were placed in U.S. cash equivalents and prime non-U.S. certificates of deposit. Luis estimates that the family's annual income needs should be about $400,000 before taxes; he understands that he and Inez will pay U.S. taxes as if they were already U.S. citizens.

Ramez has told Lindell that he had been attracted to Dexter Associates because of its reputation for economic forecasting. He is particularly concerned about protecting the purchasing power of the family assets. In the Philippines, he had suffered severe capital losses twice—once as the result of rapid inflation, and once as the result of depression. He does not want to have to rebuild the family's asset base a third time. He also wants to retain the ability to raise large amounts of cash quickly and to hold 5 percent of his portfolio in precious metals.

The Task

Lindell reviews her notes before preparing her recommendations on an investment policy and asset allocation for the Ramez portfolio. She is confident that some level of international exposure would be appropriate for the Ramez portfolio, so she also plans to present an analysis of possible international equity managers. Exhibit 2 contains performance data on three such managers.

Exhibit 2

Manager Performance Data

	Annual Rates of Return					Average Currency Component of Return
	Year 1	Year 2	Year 3	Year 4	Year 5	
Manager A	17%	24%	5%	34%	22%	60%
Manager B	−12	26	10	55	62	20
Manager C	5	28	12	50	45	40
EAFE Index	−1	25	7	56	68	20
S&P 500 Index	22	23	6	32	18	0

Because this is her first truly international client, Lindell wants to do the best job possible. She plans to start with the investment policy statement then move into asset allocation and the question of international managers.

The Ramez Family (B)

Shortly after her annual meeting with the Ramez family, Lindell found herself preparing for yet another meeting. After three years of retirement, Luis Ramez has joined a privately held international investment group specializing in global mineral extraction. Ramez is now contemplating investing $5 million for a royalty interest in an Australian oil field. He expects that his return on this investment will approximate $1.5 million a year, and petroleum engineers have projected a 10-year productive life based upon current technology. The field's production will be sold under contract to a major international oil refiner.

Lindell is concerned about how well this investment fits into the investment policy developed initially for the Ramez family. A commitment this large—42 percent of the now $12 million portfolio—violates proper diversification rules. Furthermore, she has no information on the riskiness of the royalty payments. If they materialize, they will provide far more income than needed to meet the Ramez family's present needs of $425,000 a year.

Regardless of Lindell's opinion on the matter, she knows she must prepare for the possibility that Ramez will withdraw $5 million from the existing portfolio by developing a plan to accommodate that eventuality. In preparation for a second meeting with Ramez, Lindell identifies two issues she must resolve:

- Can the existing investment policy accommodate such an investment? If not, how should the policy be modified?
- What, if any, asset allocation revision would she recommend if Ramez makes the investment and if the expected royalty level materializes?

Ednam Products Company

Faye Trotter, Assistant Treasurer of Ednam Products Company, is contemplating recent changes in the firm's pension program; its defined-benefit retirement plan has been terminated recently in favor of a new profit-sharing retirement plan. Ednam designated Trotter as the staff person responsible for the transition. Her job is to provide the profit-sharing plan participants with information on capital market expectations and the fundamentals of investing. Trotter realizes, however, that participants will also want advice on the allocation of their money among the plan's investment alternatives.

The Profit-Sharing Plan

Ednam's new profit-sharing plan is a defined-contribution plan in which each employee is responsible for investment decisions in his or her own personal account. Trotter is to provide employees with investment information, but the company is not responsible for the success or failure of an employee's investments. Under the previous, defined-benefit plan, the company made the investment decisions and ensured that plan assets were sufficient to pay for promised benefits.

Proceeds from the termination of the defined-benefit plan were used to purchase for each employee an annuity covering accrued benefits up to the termination date. Before termination, Ednam also had sponsored a generous savings plan under which many employees had accumulated sizable participations. These accumulations were incorporated into the employees' individual accounts as an integral part of the new plan. The new plan is fully qualified under the Employee Retirement Income Security Act (ERISA) and meets all requirements for protecting employee tax benefits that are part of this type of arrangement.

The plan makes six no-load mutual funds available for employee investments:
- *Money Market Fund.* Average maturity of 30 days. Current yield is 7 percent.
- *High-Grade Bond Fund.* Average maturity of 15 years. Current yield is 11 percent.
- *Domestic Stock Fund.* An S&P 500 proxy. Current yield is 3 percent.
- *Small-Capitalization Stock Fund.* Current yield is 1 percent.
- *International Stock Fund.* A Europe, Australia, Far East (EAFE) proxy. Current yield is 2 percent.
- *Equity Real Estate Fund.* Current yield is 7 percent.

Participating employees must make all investment decisions for their own personal accounts. They must select among the investment vehicles offered, dispose of the accumulated monies now awaiting investment, monitor and adjust their account exposures, and allocate future profit-sharing contributions by the company.

Employees cannot withdraw funds from their accounts until retirement, normally at age 65. At retirement, employees have the option of taking a lump-sum distribution of the proceeds or rolling the assets over into an IRA. Employees may invest their IRAs in the six funds offered by the plan. Distributions from the plan are taxable, but rolling over the plan assets into an IRA has no tax consequences until the funds are withdrawn. Employees are required to begin taking distributions from their IRAs at age 70½, if they have not already done so. Trotter is preparing a memo on the specific options available to employees upon retirement.

The employees have been told that retirement fund investing requires their continuing participation, with particular attention to adjustment in market exposures as their personal and external conditions change.

The Task

Ednam management knows that this decision-making requirement is a totally new experience for most employees. Many have expressed concern about this new requirement, and Trotter expects a flood of employees through her office in the next few weeks. To prepare for the variety of expected questions, Trotter selects for analysis four management-level employees. Using information from the sign-up forms these employees submitted (see Exhibit 1), Trotter plans to draw up investment policy guidelines and an appropriate asset mix for each of them. She believes the experience gained through this exercise will prepare her for the challenges of advising the entire staff.

Exhibit 1

Excerpts from Data Forms

Margaret Custer, Assistant Director of Market Research. Age 30. Single. Excellent health. Buying a $70,000 condominium (heavily mortgaged) and a car. Salary is $25,000. Accumulated in plan investment account: $20,000.

Glenn Abbott, Plant Supervisor. Age 42. Widower; two children, ages 14 and 10. Buying a $100,000 house ($75,000 mortgage). No other indebtedness except regular heavy use of credit cards. Savings of $25,000. Salary is $40,000. Accumulated in plan investment account: $90,000.

Tom Davis, Sales Manager. Age 58. Intends to retire at age 62. Married; no children; wife employed. Owns $135,000 house (no mortgage), $50,000 in an IRA (which is currently invested in a small-cap stock fund), $50,000 in bank CDs, and a $100,000 portfolio of growth stocks. No family health problems; no major indebtedness. Salary is $60,000. Accumulated in plan investment account: $160,000.

Pete Jones, Production Manager. Age 64. Intends to retire at age 65, in six months. Married; no children; wife is not employed. Owns $150,000 house (no mortgage), $100,000 in an IRA (which is currently invested in a short-term bond fund), $100,000 in bank CDs, and a $125,000 portfolio of "blue chip" stocks. No family health problems; no major indebtedness. Salary is $70,000. Accumulated in plan investment account: $225,000.

Trotter also reviews a brokerage firm's report detailing capital market expectations for the next five years. The report predicts that the level of risk and return for the asset classes will be in line with average historical experience and that a more-or-less normal economic environment will be accompanied by modest inflation levels. Trotter feels comfortable with these expectations and proceeds to compose an appropriate investment policy and asset mix for each of the four employees.

Mid-South Trucking Company

Fred Smith, CFA, a portfolio manager for a large investment advisory firm, is reviewing background information on Mid-South Trucking Company. John Oliver, formerly a senior partner of a management consulting firm and the recently elected president of Mid-South, has learned that Mid-South's defined-benefit pension plan is invested 100 percent in bonds, with a maximum maturity of 10 years. Oliver believes that "anyone can buy bonds and sit on them" and that "a pension plan should be managed so as to maximize return within well-defined risk parameters." He has requested that Smith, as an informed and objective observer, advise him on possible changes in the plan's asset mix.

The Company

Mid-South is the eighth largest domestic trucking company, with annual revenues of $850 million. Revenues have grown about 8 percent a year for the past five years, with one down year. The company employs about 7,000 people, and its annual payroll approximates $300 million. The average age of the workforce is 43 years. Company profits last year were $20 million, compared to $12 million five years ago.

The Pension Plan

Mid-South's defined-benefit plan was established in 1965. The company annually contributes 7 percent of payroll to fund the plan. During the past five years, portfolio income has covered payments for retirees, and company contributions have been available for investment. Although the plan is currently adequately funded, unfunded past service liabilities are equal to 40 percent of plan assets. This liability is being funded over the next 35 years. Plan assets are valued annually on a rolling four-year average for actuarial purposes. The current portfolio is presented in Exhibit 1.

Although actual plan results have averaged 10 percent a year for the past 20 years, for purposes of this analysis, Mid-South's management, in consultation with the actuary, has decided to use an assumed annual rate of 7 percent. (FAS 87 requires annual reassessment of the assumed rate of return.) Based on past company experience, wages and salaries are assumed to increase 5 percent a year.

The Task

Before the meeting, Smith reviews his firm's latest investment projections. Al-

Exhibit 1

Current Portfolio
(dollars in millions)

	Cost	Market Value	Current Yield	Yield to Maturity
Cash equivalents	$ 10	$ 10	5.8%	5.8%
Treasury notes (1 year)	25	25	6.5	6.4
Treasury notes (2-7 yrs.)	110	115	8.0	7.8
Treasury bonds (7-10 yrs.)	115	127	8.8	8.5
Total	$260	$278		

though continued prosperity is considered the most likely outlook for the next three to five years, two alternatives have been allowed for: a return to high inflation, or a move into deflation/depression. Exhibit 2 presents the details of the projections.

Exhibit 2

Capital Market Outlook
Three- to Five-Year Projections

	Expected Annual Return	Expected Annual Yield
Continued prosperity **(60% probability)**		
Cash equivalents	6.0%	7.0%
Domestic stocks	12.0	4.0
Treasury bonds	8.0	13.0
High inflation **(25% probability)**		
Cash equivalents	10.0%	7.0%
Domestic stocks	15.0	5.0
Treasury bonds	3.0	16.0
Deflation/depression **(15% probability)**		
Cash equivalents	2.0%	7.0%
Domestic stocks	–6.0	3.0
Domestic bonds	12.0	10.0

Smith is to prepare an investment policy statement appropriate for the Mid-South Trucking Company's plan and recommend changes to the existing all-bond asset allocation. He feels that this recommendation should be limited to domestic stocks, domestic bonds, and cash equivalents, deferring discussion of other asset classes and instruments to a later date.

General Technology Corporation (A)

The Board of Directors of General Technology Corporation (GTC) recently decided to change the way GTC's pension and profit-sharing retirement plans are invested.[1] The Board has selected John Irish, CFA, an independent investment advisor, to provide counsel and assistance during the transition period to Alfred Darwin, Vice President—Finance, and the company's new Investment Committee.

The Company
General Technology Corporation is a successful, 10-year-old concern that is beginning to mature in its organizational aspects. Up to now, it has used annuity contracts to fund its retirement plan. A major insurance company provides all investment-related needs other than periodic policy reviews, allowing GTC's small finance staff to focus on the company's rapid expansion rather than retirement plan investments. This arrangement has produced satisfactory results, largely because interest rates during the company's 10-year life have exceeded the pension plan's actuarial requirement.

Now, however, the company needs to be more responsive to the benefit requirements of its expanded work force. Accordingly, its directors have decided to "unbundle" the retirement plan's assets and withdraw from the all-annuity format in favor of separate pension and profit-sharing portfolios. The pension portfolio will be managed by several investment counselors; each participant in the profit-sharing plan will allocate his or her own holdings in that plan among five mutual fund investment alternatives. Darwin supervises the planning, policy-making, and objective-setting activities related to the new structure.

Darwin informs Irish that the Directors have a conservative attitude toward risk taking and explains that this is the company's first experience with separately invested portfolios, which will be permitted to hold domestic stocks, equity real estate, cash equivalents, and domestic bonds. Darwin also tells Irish that the Investment Committee's outlook, while divided, leans toward expectations of below-normal business growth and steady or slowly declining inflation for several years. The pension fund has an 8.5 percent annual required rate of return.

The Presentation
The GTC Board asks Irish to make a presentation explaining the attractiveness of different asset classes under two economic scenarios, one of which the Investment

---

[1]The profit-sharing plan is addressed in the Profit-Sharing Advisory, Inc. cases, pp. 33-35.

Committee provided. Also, he is to write an investment policy statement and recommend an asset allocation for the pension portfolio.

Irish prepares a set of probabilities for various possible economic environments under two sets of expectations—one that reflects the view of the Investment Committee, and another suggesting a "return-to-inflation," as predicted by several economists. The two forecasts, based on a three-year time frame, are shown in Exhibit 1. Exhibit 2 shows expected returns and standard deviations (derived from

Exhibit 1

Economic Outlook
(Probability Values)

	Investment Committee View	Return-to-Inflation View
Higher growth, lower inflation	15%	10%
Higher growth, higher inflation	21	30
Lower growth, higher inflation	22	40
Lower growth, lower inflation	22	10
Accelerating inflation	5	6
Deflation	15	4

Exhibit 2

Capital Market Outlook
Three-Year Projections

	Investment Committee View		Return-to-Inflation View		Historical Data	
	Expected Annual Return	Standard Deviation	Expected Annual Return	Standard Deviation	Actual Annual Return	Standard Deviation
Domestic stocks	19.9%	12.6%	24.1%	18.3%	10.2%	15.6%
Domestic bonds	20.4	5.8	17.3	5.8	8.2	2.8
Cash equivalents	11.0	3.7	12.8	3.0	6.4	2.8
Equity real estate	7.0	6.6	11.1	4.3	12.4	1.8
Inflation rate	6.2	4.3	8.1	2.7	5.0	3.4
Real GNP growth	3.0	2.2	3.1	1.5	3.2	2.8

information in Exhibit 1). Exhibit 3 presents the expected correlations among asset-class returns and economic variables. To support his conclusion—and to make sure the board understands the risks and potential returns associated with each portfolio—Irish plans to discuss the investment implications of the two economic scenarios, highlighting the expected performance of different asset classes under each scenario.

Exhibit 3

Expected Correlations

	Cash Equivalents	Domestic Stocks	Domestic Bonds	Equity Real Estate	Inflation
Cash equivalents	1.00				
Domestic stocks	0.50	1.00			
Domestic bonds	–0.96	–0.30	1.00		
Equity real estate	0.90	0.71	–0.80	1.00	
Inflation rate	0.88	0.69	–0.77	0.99	1.00
Real GNP growth	0.62	0.94	–0.42	0.86	0.87

Irish has identified six possible asset allocation alternatives, shown in Exhibit 4. Now, he must select the one that best meets the objectives and constraints outlined in the investment policy statement.

Exhibit 4

Asset Mix Alternatives

Asset Mix	Domestic Stocks	Domestic Bonds	Cash Equivalents	Equity Real Estate
1	30%	50%	0%	20%
2	20	70	10	0
3	55	35	5	5
4	10	80	0	10
5	70	20	5	5
6	45	50	5	0

General Technology Corporation (B)

Irish's presentation to the Board was well received. The Board adopted his recommendation, and the portfolio has performed well. Since then, Darwin has consulted Irish each time the Investment Committee has changed its view.

Yesterday, Darwin asked Irish for more advice. At the Investment Committee meeting the day before, the chairman had voiced new concerns about the economy. The Committee had revised its views to those shown in Exhibit 1 and also had reduced the required rate of return for the company's pension plan from 8.5 percent to 6 percent. No change was made to the correlation matrix. Darwin believes that these changes will require a new asset mix, but he wants Irish's advice. He also wants Irish to help justify any change in asset mix to the Board.

Exhibit 1
Revised and Original Investment Committee Views

	Revised View		Original View	
	Expected Annual Return	Standard Deviation	Expected Annual Return	Standard Deviation
Domestic stocks	9.0%	18.9%	19.9%	12.6%
Domestic bonds	6.4	5.6	20.4	5.8
Cash equivalents	3.5	2.0	11.0	3.7
Equity real estate	4.5	9.0	7.0	6.6
Inflation rate	2.0	1.5	6.2	4.3
Real GNP growth	2.0	1.1	3.0	2.2

Profit-Sharing Advisory, Inc. (A)

Barbara Martin, CFA, a founding partner of Profit-Sharing Advisory, Inc. (PSA), is preparing for her first meeting with a potential new client, General Technology Corporation (GTC).[1] PSA provides a full range of services to firms offering defined-contribution profit-sharing plans as part or all of their retirement programs. Alfred Darwin, GTC's Vice President—Finance, asked Martin to make a presentation to the firm's Investment Committee. He wants to know whether PSA can alleviate the confusion caused by the firm's recent decision to unbundle its retirement plan assets. Martin decided to illustrate the value-added of her services by presenting a case study focusing on one of GTC's employees, Gordon Williams.

In preparation for the upcoming meeting, Martin interviewed Williams in some detail. After this interview, she decides to contrast Williams' ideas about investment policy and asset allocation with her own recommendations. She believes this tactic will permit her to highlight the differences between the two and will clearly illustrate the benefits of her approach.

General Technology Corporation

General Technology Corporation is a successful, 10-year-old concern beginning to mature in its organizational aspects. In an effort to be more responsive to the benefit requirements of its expanded workforce, the company recently decided to withdraw from the all-annuity format of retirement plan investing in favor of separate pension and profit-sharing portfolios. The pension plan assets will be managed by several investment counselors, but individual participants in the profit-sharing plan will allocate their own assets among five mutual fund investment alternatives:

- *Growth Stock Fund.*
- *Common Stock Fund.*
- *Corporate Bond Fund.*
- *Equity Real Estate Fund.*
- *Money Market Fund.*

Darwin supervises the planning, policy-making, and objective-setting activities related to the new structure. He is most concerned about the requirement that participants allocate and periodically reallocate their own accounts among the four mutual funds. He believes that too little time is available to counsel each employee on investment policy and asset allocation decisions, and he worries that some employees might make asset allocation mistakes that could jeopardize their financial security in retirement.

---

[1] See General Technology Corporation, pp. 29-32.

Gordon Williams

Gordon Williams is GTC's Vice President—Research and Development. He is 39 years old, is married, and has three young children whose care absorbs most of his wife's time now and will for at least the next few years. The Williamses own their own home, save regularly, have adequate health and life insurance, and avoid debt beyond the usual monthly charge-card balance outstanding and a home mortgage of $80,000. Their home has a current market value of $120,000. The present balance in Williams' profit-sharing account (from which the company does not permit borrowing) is approximately $130,000. The family also has $40,000 in outside savings—$25,000 in a certificate of deposit maturing next month, $5,000 in a bank savings account, and $10,000 in GTC common stock.

Williams plans to split investments in the profit-sharing account equally between the bond fund and the equity real estate fund when the initial allocation is made at the beginning of next month. He says that he and his wife are "middle-of-the-road" people when it comes to risk taking. Williams' attempt to identify objectives, constraints, and preferences; create an investment policy; and develop an asset allocation is presented in Exhibit 1.

Exhibit 1

Williams' Plan for His Profit-Sharing Account

Investment Policy Statement
  Investment Objective
> Get as high a return as possible without taking a lot of risk. Keep up with inflation, plus a little more if possible.

  Investment Constraints
- **Time Horizon:** I don't think anyone can forecast more than about one year, at best, so a one-year time horizon is right for us. We will invest one year at a time.
- **Liquidity:** We always keep at least $5,000 in savings for emergencies.
- **Taxes:** 40 percent marginal tax rate; do not expect it to go lower.
- **Regulatory/Legal:** Cannot think of any problems here.
- **Unique Preferences and Circumstances:** Just what we have already told you about our personal financial situation and "middle-of-the-road" attitudes.

Asset Allocation
> Split the $130,000 profit-sharing account equally between domestic bonds and equity real estate to get an average exposure.

The Presentation

Martin believes she can devise a better investment policy and asset allocation than Williams has on his own. She plans to use historical capital market returns to develop an appropriate presentation for the upcoming meeting with GTC.

Profit-Sharing Advisory, Inc. (B)

Martin's presentation was enthusiastically received. Darwin was confident she could provide the up-front advisory services that the firm wants to offer its employees. Darwin hired Martin and encouraged all employees to attend an informational meeting with her. Williams was one of the first employees in line.

With the passage of time and several new developments, Williams' circumstances changed, causing him to doubt that the existing allocation of his account is still appropriate. Because of the recent death of a relative, he became the beneficiary of a trust that is expected to provide him with $50,000 of taxable income in each of the next 25 years. At the end of this time, the trust will terminate and the assets will go to a charitable organization; Williams will receive no further benefits from the trust. Williams plans to continue at his present job and foresees no radical change in his family's basic goals or lifestyle as a result of this new development, except that he can breath easier about the costs of educating his children.

Martin agrees to meet with Williams on the following Friday. In preparation for the meeting, she rereads Williams' file. He certainly is fortunate, she mused. Of course, this change in circumstances would affect his investment policy and asset allocation. She sets about writing up the revisions she considers necessary.

Industrial Products Corporation (A)

The management of Industrial Products Corporation (IPC), a publicly held company, plans to take the company private in hopes of improving IPC's operating and financial performance. Management intends to take IPC public again in about five years. The only remaining detail is the development of a post-buyout investment policy for IPC's defined-benefit retirement plan. Tom Luck, CFA, a senior member of the management team, has been assigned this task.

The company's employees are unionized but agree to support the buyout and to accept lower future salary increases and a reduced work force in return for a significant increase in retirement benefit levels. The employees' union wants to participate in formulating future policy for the pension fund because the wage concessions have increased the importance of the expected pension benefits. Indeed, their expected pension benefits represent the major asset of most IPC employees.

Even after considering the higher level of retirement benefits to be paid after the buyout, the pension plan currently is well funded. Management opposes employee involvement in setting pension investment policy but agrees to hear the union's proposals at a meeting in which it will also present its own policy ideas.

One of management's goals after the buyout is for the company to become the industry's low-cost producer. Despite the higher basic future benefit level, management wants to reduce total pension expense under FAS 87 by aggressively seeking high pension portfolio returns. Company contributions and portfolio income at about a 3 percent current yield level are expected to approximate pension payouts during the next five years.

Management agrees to limit its salary compensation during the post-buyout period. If it succeeds in improving the company's operating and financial performance during this period, key management personnel should realize substantial profits upon going public again.

Because of the importance of the pension plan in the buyout, Luck wants to address all critical issues and justify all recommendations, anticipating that extensive discussion would precede any final decisions. Luck plans to begin with the investment policy statement.

Industrial Products Corporation (B)

As Luck anticipated, the union representative, Marilyn Jones, objected to some aspects of the management proposal. The meeting was adjourned for one week so that the union could prepare a counterproposal. Jones now has the task of revising management's investment policy ideas to represent the needs of the employees better. The union's primary objective is to maximize future retirement benefit security, but this objective conflicts with management's desire to reduce pension expenses by maximizing future pension fund investment returns.

To strengthen its position in other areas of negotiation, the union has agreed to accept annual real wage increases of 1 percent, rather than the historical rate of 3 percent. The union insisted, however, that this concession be contingent on management's agreement to introduce annual post-retirement cost-of-living increases equal to the inflation rate. Jones believes that this requirement is not onerous, because the actual numbers of retirees will be small for the next several years. Jones proceeds to revise the investment policy statement to reflect this point of view.

Industrial Products Corporation (C)

Luck has learned that management accepted the union's proposal, including the inflation-indexed cost-of-living adjustment of future pension benefits, and agreed to a less aggressive investment approach. Jones' investment policy statement and her suggested asset allocation, shown below, were rejected, however.

Union's Proposed Asset Allocation

Domestic bonds, long-term	60%
Domestic stocks	25
Cash equivalents	10
Equity real estate	3
International stocks	2

Luck believes that Jones and the union could reach an agreement with management if each side would accept a toned-down approach to investment of the pension fund for at least the next five years. He devises an asset allocation that would satisfy the union's policy preferences and yet largely preserve management's goal of high investment returns. He knows he will have to explain how his proposal can benefit each side, as well as how the presence of inflation-indexed benefit obligations (IBOs) in the retirement package would affect the plan's asset allocation.

Universal Products, Inc.

The Directors' Planning Committee of Universal Products, Inc. (UPI) recently completed a detailed study of the intermediate-term outlook for the business. Based on inputs from a wide range of external consulting sources, as well as from UPI's own economics department, the study forecasts 18 to 24 months of good conditions ahead, followed by a sharp and deep recession giving way to stagflation, possibly for the subsequent four years. Exhibit 1 presents the study's GNP forecasts, inflation outlook, and interest rate predictions for the next six years.

Exhibit 1
Planning Committee's Forecast

	Annual Change in Real GNP	*Annual Inflation Rate*	*Annual Yield Levels*	
			Treasury Bills	*30-Year Treasuries*
Current	4.0%	3.0%	8.0%	8.5%
1 year hence	2.5	5.0	9.0	9.5
2 years hence	–2.0	1.5	5.5	8.0
3 years hence	–8.5	–4.0	2.5	4.5
4 years hence	–1.0	2.0	3.0	5.5
5 years hence	–0.5	3.5	6.5	8.5
6 years hence	1.5	6.5	9.5	10.0

The company has revised its business plan to reflect this economic outlook and is reviewing its entire financial operations. It anticipates some work force shrinkage. Jack Jenson, Assistant Treasurer, must consider the effect of this forecast on UPI's two retirement plan portfolios. He must also determine whether to include equity real estate as an asset class for these portfolios.

UPI Retirement Plans

UPI has a defined-benefit pension plan and a defined-contribution profit-sharing plan, both of which are managed in-house. The existing asset allocation of these portfolios appears in Exhibit 2. Both plans are ERISA-qualified and tax-exempt.

The company has a relatively mature work force. The pension plan, though modestly overfunded, is approaching the point at which all of the company's annual

Exhibit 2

Existing Asset Allocations
(dollars in thousands)

	Pension Portfolio		Profit-Sharing Portfolio	
Cash equivalents	$ 500	0.5%	$ 250	0.5%
Domestic bonds	16,000	14.5	8,000	14.5
Domestic stocks	93,500	85.0	46,750	85.0
Total	$110,000	100.0%	$55,000	100.0%

contribution, plus normal portfolio income, will be needed to meet benefit payments to retired workers; little or no excess income will be available for reinvestment.

A participant in the profit-sharing plan can withdraw his or her vested interest only in the event of termination, involuntary early retirement, or normal retirement at age 65. Participants rely on the company to allocate and invest the assets appropriately; no provision exists for participant-designated individual investment choices. Company policy limits investments to three asset classes—domestic stocks, domestic bonds, and cash equivalents—a restricting influence that Jenson would like to eliminate. Both retirement plan portfolios are very heavily growth oriented and have realized especially favorable returns for the past several years.

The Economic Forecast

As the planning study reveals, Jenson will confront two very different investment climates in planning the retirement portfolios for the next five years. Although positive conditions are expected to continue for up to 24 months, implications for the following four years are heavily negative.

The current period of business expansion has extended an unusually long time. Jenson is not surprised by the prospect of a cyclical peak within the next two years. He is concerned, however, about the expectation of a steep post-peak economic decline, a lengthy period of sluggish business, and inflation rising beyond normal business cycle experience.

Jenson places a 50 percent probability on the Planning Committee's forecast for the next six years, but he believes that another course of events is equally likely. This possibility involves a milder recession and a shorter, less inflation-plagued period of subnormal business activity before recovery begins (see Exhibit 3).

Exhibit 4 presents information concerning current capital market conditions.

The Task

Jenson must review UPI's present investment policy and make recommendations

Exhibit 3
Jenson's Alternative Forecast

	Annual Change in Real GNP	Annual Inflation Rate	Annual Yield Level	
			Treasury Bills	30-Year Treasuries
Current	4.0%	3.0%	8.0%	8.5%
1 year hence	3.0	4.0	9.0	9.5
2 years hence	1.5	2.0	6.5	8.5
3 years hence	−2.0	0.0	4.0	6.5
4 years hence	−0.5	1.0	6.0	8.0
5 years hence	1.5	2.5	6.5	8.5
6 years hence	3.0	3.5	8.0	9.5

Exhibit 4
Current Capital Markets Data

S&P 500 Index			Interest Rates		
P/E Ratio	Price-to-Book Value	Dividend Yield	Treasury Bills	30-Year Treasuries	Equity Risk Premium
20.5X	2.10X	2.00%	8.00%	8.50%	150 basis pts.

to the Planning Committee in two weeks. His main task is to prepare a revised investment policy statement and a revised asset allocation for each of the plans. He also must discuss equity real estate as an investment alternative for the pension and the profit-sharing portfolios. In the past, UPI's sales, profit margin, earnings, and other business trends have closely tracked those of the entire U.S. manufacturing sector. This pattern is very much on Jenson's mind as he prepares for the meeting. The company's president and several other members of the Planning Committee are also members of the Retirement Committee, to which Jenson reports, so Jenson knows he must defend his recommendations with facts and sound logic.

World Ecosystem Consortium (A)

Ernest Nimrod, CFA, is an independent advisor to the Benefit and Investment Committee of World Ecosystem Consortium (WEC). He has been engaged to provide counsel on investment policy and asset allocation. WEC is a quasi-governmental organization sanctioned by several countries to conduct environmental research on their behalf. WEC's Board of Directors has instructed this newly formed committee to conduct a critical review of the investment practices of WEC's tax-exempt, defined-benefit pension trust. Under the terms of its international charter, WEC operates under the same rules and regulations as a U.S. corporation and is not subject to additional investment or accounting regulations by any other countries where it has employees or operations.

The WEC Pension Trust

The pension trust is well funded by virtually any measure, and WEC intends to maintain it in that condition. Although headquartered in the United States, WEC has employees in many parts of the world; in fact, as shown below, more than half of its currently projected benefit liabilities are payable in various non-U.S. currencies.

Currency	Percent of Total Benefit Liabilities
United States	40%
Canada	20
Japan	10
Singapore	10
United Kingdom	5
Switzerland	5
Other non-U.S. currencies	10

Reflecting a decade of rapid expansion, many of WEC's employees are relatively young and have less than 10 years of service; active employees outnumber retirees by more than three to one. Because of WEC's policy of conservative funding, contributions to the pension fund and its annual income exceed payments to retirees by a comfortable margin. WEC's actuary projects that this condition will persist for at least another 10 years under current funding policy.

Because WEC's operations in Canada were among the first established, its Canadian work force has a much older profile than that of WEC as a whole. Retired employees outnumber active employees by two to one, and pension payments are significantly larger than current pension expenses for active Canadian workers.

The formula WEC uses to determine a retiree's pension benefit is based on the retiring individual's average salary during his or her years of service and the number of years of service (the "career-average" method). The benefit thus calculated is the retiree's fixed annual pension payment. WEC has never augmented these fixed payments to reflect inflation or any other nonsalary or service-related factors.

The Task
Nimrod must create an investment policy statement for WEC's pension trust. Once this is done, he will recommend an appropriate asset allocation for the trust.

World Ecosystem Consortium (B)

After making his initial recommendations, Nimrod learns that the Benefit and Investment Committee is concerned about the severe loss of purchasing power that WEC retirees have experienced in the past and is considering a major change in the benefit formula. It proposes to use final-year salary instead of career-average salary in calculating pension benefits; all other aspects of the formula would remain unchanged. The committee is also considering adoption of an "unwritten policy" dictum that would obligate WEC to make ad hoc retirement benefit increases whenever future inflation rates reach "high levels."

The Committee has asked Nimrod for his guidance. In particular, the members want to know what repercussions the benefit formula change and the "unwritten policy" dictum might have on the investment policy and on asset allocation.

Good Samaritan Hospital (A)

Mr. P.V. Wise, CFA, a portfolio manager at Investment Associates, is preparing for a meeting with Mary Atkins to discuss her portfolio. Wise has just learned that Atkins has been diagnosed as having a terminal illness and is not expected to live for more than nine months. Wise expects this news to affect the investment of her portfolio and notes that her investment policy statement should be updated.

Mary Atkins

Mary Atkins, age 66, became a client of Investment Associates five years ago upon the death of her husband, Charles Atkins. Mr. Atkins had owned a successful newspaper business, which he sold two years before his death to Merit Enterprises, a publishing and broadcasting conglomerate, in exchange for shares of Merit common stock. Atkins had believed that Merit had a bright future and requested that the stock be retained, if possible. Although Mrs. Atkins had consented to sell some Merit shares to provide better portfolio diversification, the remaining Merit holding still represents a large percentage of her portfolio's total value.

The Atkins portfolio has a market value of $2 million. Recent sales of Merit stock generated a $50,000 capital gain. The portfolio currently produces $118,200 of annual income, more then half of which is exempt from federal income taxes. Mrs. Atkins also receives substantial income from a life annuity purchased before Mr. Atkins' death. This income level allows Mrs. Atkins to live comfortably, although her income has not kept pace with inflation during the past five years. Fortunately, she is covered adequately by medical insurance.

The Atkinses had no children. Their wills provide that the assets remaining after Mrs. Atkins' death be used to create the Atkins Endowment Fund for the benefit of Good Samaritan Hospital. Because her life expectancy is less than a year, Mrs. Atkins wants to make sure that her financial affairs are in order. She looks forward to the meeting with Investment Associates, expecting that they can devise a portfolio that satisfies her immediate financial needs, as well as the future needs of the Good Samaritan Hospital.

Good Samaritan Hospital

Good Samaritan is a 180-bed, not-for-profit hospital with an annual operating budget of $12.5 million. Until five years ago, the hospital's operating revenues were sufficient to meet operating expenses and even to generate an occasional small surplus. More recently, however, rising costs and declining occupancy rates are causing Good Samaritan to incur operating deficits averaging $350,000 annually.

As a result, the hospital's Board of Governors decided to increase the endowment's current investment income objective from 5 percent to 6 percent of total assets in order to reduce the size of the deficit.

The market value of Good Samaritan's existing endowment assets is $7.5 million. The portfolio generates approximately $375,000 of income annually, up from less than $200,000 five years ago. This increased income resulted from higher interest rates and a shift in asset mix toward more bonds. The new 6 percent requirement will raise investment income to approximately $450,000 yearly.

The hospital has not received any significant additions to its endowment assets in the past five years.

The Immediate Task

Wise has reviewed Atkins' original, five-year-old investment policy statement (Exhibit 1) and the current portfolio (Exhibit 2) for the account in preparation for the meeting with Mrs. Atkins. He intends to write a new investment policy statement and to recommend specific investment actions that should be taken in the near future. He plans to articulate for Mrs. Atkins the justification for each action.

Exhibit 1

Original Investment Policy Statement for Mrs. Atkins

Objectives

Return Requirements: Mrs. Atkins requires a minimum of $50,000 after-tax investment income annually. Future investment income growth should attempt to keep pace with inflation. Given the fact that the assets will go to a charitable remainderman eventually, capital growth is also needed.

Risk Tolerance: Mrs. Atkins can assume modest risk to achieve income growth, provided that her minimum income need (adjusted for future inflation) is met. If the size of the fund builds over time, somewhat increased risk could be incurred to facilitate growth of capital.

Constraints

Liquidity: Because death taxes have been provided for and the assets will go to an endowment at her death, liquidity needs are low, except for any related to investment considerations.

Time Horizon: Mrs. Atkins's shorter-than-average personal time horizon is not an important investment consideration because her wealth will go to an endowment fund, which has an infinite time horizon, on her death.

Laws and Regulations: Because this is a personal portfolio, regulatory and legal constraints are not significant investment factors; Prudent Man rules apply.

Tax Considerations: Mrs. Atkins is in the highest income tax bracket and would benefit from appropriate tax-advantaged investments.

Policy

The following guidelines were developed and approved following agreement between Investment Associates and Mrs. Atkins on the above objectives and constraints:

Asset Allocation:
50 to 70% - Domestic stocks and issues convertible into domestic stocks.
20 to 50% - Fixed-income investments, principally tax-exempt.
0 to 20% - Short-term reserves, principally tax-exempt.

Diversification: With the exception of Merit Enterprises, individual common stock (and common stock equivalent) holdings should not exceed $50,000 at cost or $100,000 at market. Individual fixed-income holdings should not exceed $100,000 at cost or $150,000 at market.

Quality Criteria: All convertible securities and debt instruments must be rated no less than BBB as defined by Standard & Poor's, or its equivalent as defined by other rating agencies. All domestic stocks must have a history of at least five years of continuous dividend payment.

Exhibit 2
Investment Portfolio of Mrs. Atkins

		Recent Price	Market Value	Cost Basis	Annual Income
Shares	*Domestic Stocks*				
20,220	Merit Enterprises	$39	$788,600	$475,000	$24,800
1,000	Caterpillar Tractor	32	32,000	50,000	500
1,000	General Electric	58	58,000	50,000	2,000
500	IBM	122	61,000	38,000	2,200
2,000	Penn Power & Light	24	48,000	40,000	5,000
1,000	Standard Oil of Indiana	57	57,000	49,000	3,000
1,300	Weyerhauser	28	36,400	49,000	1,700
			$1,081,000	$751,000	$39,200
Par Value	*Convertible Issues*				
$50,000	John Deere 9% bonds due 2008	98	$49,000	$50,000	$4,500
$50,000	American Medical 13% bonds due 2001	140	70,000	50,000	6,500
			$119,000	$100,000	$11,000
Par Value	*Municipal Bonds*				
$100,000	Albuquerque, NM School Bonds 6.6% due 6/15/91	92	$92,000	$100,000	$6,600
$100,000	Cincinnati, OH GO 10% due 12/1/92	101	101,000	100,000	10,000
$100,000	Illinois State GO 8.6% due 10/1/95	101	101,000	100,000	8,600
$100,000	Lynchburg, VA GO 7.5% due 6/1/91	93	93,000	100,000	7,500
$100,000	Oregon State GO 8.2% due 2/1/91	89	89,000	100,000	8,200
$100,000	Sacramento, CA Util. Rev. Bonds 11.0% due 5/1/94	108	108,000	100,000	11,000
$100,000	Sheboygan, WI GO 10.20% due 4/1/91	106	106,000	100,000	10,200
			$690,000	$700,000	$62,100
Market Value	*Short-Term Reserves*				
$110,000	Tax-exempt money market fund	1	$ 110,000	$ 110,000	$ 5,900
	Total portfolio		$2,000,000	$1,661,000	$118,200

Good Samaritan Hospital (B)

Before Wise was able to take any of the investment actions identified for discussion at the pending meeting, Mrs. Atkins died and title to the assets passed to the hospital's Board of Governors. The Board announced that it would select a manager for the Atkins Endowment Fund from among four firms with experience in managing endowment portfolios. It would leave the portfolio with Investment Associates temporarily, but it requested that major purchases or sales be deferred until the manager decision has been made and an appropriate investment policy has been adopted.

Investment Associates is one of the four firms under consideration. Wise now has the task of preparing for a presentation to the Board of Good Samaritan Hospital. Wanting an expression of investment philosophy for endowment funds, the Board requested that each firm address the following issues in its presentation:

1. Prepare an Investment Policy statement for the Atkins Endowment Fund, taking into account all relevant objectives and constraints.
2. What immediate changes, if any, would you recommend for the Atkins portfolio pending the selection of a new portfolio manager?
3. Assume that your firm is selected as the new manager for the fund. Disregarding Good Samaritan's other endowment assets and basing your answer on the economic and capital market expectations supplied by the Board of Governors (Exhibit 1), what specific actions would you take?

Exhibit 1

Good Samaritan Hospital Board of Governors
Twelve-Month Forecast

Economic Expectations

	Forecast	Range
Real GNP	3.5%	3.0 to 4.0%
Inflation	4.7	4.0 to 5.5

Capital Market Expectations

	Current Annual Yield Level	Expected Annual Return	Standard Deviation of Return
Domestic stocks	4.2%	22.5%	25.2%
Domestic bonds	11.7	19.4	18.4
Cash equivalents	9.0	8.6	2.2

Good Samaritan Hospital (C)

After a hiatus of nearly four months, Investment Associates has been notified that it is being retained to manage the Atkins Endowment Fund on behalf of Good Samaritan Hospital. Realizing that new investment actions may be in order, Wise gathers the firm's report on economic and capital market expectations (Exhibit 1) and prepares to make his recommendations. He also prepares himself to explain why his current recommendations differ from those presented to the Board at the earlier meeting.

Exhibit 1

**Investor Associates
Twelve-Month Forecast**

Economic Expectations

	Forecast	*Range*
Real GNP	4.1%	3.5 to 4.9%
Inflation	5.9	5.0 to 6.9

Capital Market Expectations

	Current Annual Yield Level	*Expected Annual Return*	*Standard Deviation of Return*
Domestic stocks (S&P 500)	3.8%	11.9%	17.4%
Domestic bonds	11.2	10.5	9.7
Cash equivalents	7.0	8.6	2.1

Guideline Answers

The Mason Family (A)

This case illustrates the main considerations involved in setting investment policy and determining asset allocation for individuals. In this instance, the life-cycle approach must be adapted to suit the unique circumstances of the client. The Masons are a couple near retirement who are about to receive a large infusion of capital ($1 million) and expect a substantial royalty income stream in future years. Investment policy should reflect the fact that the family's demand for income from the investments would change if and as the royalty income becomes more certain. Thus, the time horizon has two parts: the first year or two, and then a longer time period representing the life expectancy of the Masons. Assets in this case include only domestic stocks and bonds and cash equivalents.

Investment Policy
Investment policy for the Masons must express their investment objectives and consider all relevant constraints on the achievement of these objectives.

Objectives
Return Requirements: The rate of return on the Mason's assets must provide them with adequate retirement income, on an inflation-adjusted basis. In addition, the return on their assets should be large enough to allow them some financial participation in their grandchildren's education. Income from the portfolio should be sufficient in the first year to replace Dr. Mason's Essex salary and provide additional money for the Masons' other objectives. To the extent that royalty income materializes later, it can provide most or all of the Masons' income requirements; at that time, the portfolio should be shifted to a growth orientation.

Risk Tolerance: The portfolio should accept only a low-to-moderate level of risk to reduce the volatility of the portfolio. The Masons are entering retirement with a $1 million portfolio, plus the equity in their home, as financial assets. One of the objectives of the portfolio is to preserve this capital base. Although the Masons expect substantial royalty income, this might not materialize or might stop suddenly. Thus, the portfolio should retain sufficient liquidity to meet the need for flexibility during the first year.

Constraints
Liquidity: After the first year or so, if royalties develop, liquidity is not a major requirement for the Masons' portfolio.

Time Horizon: A medium-long time horizon is appropriate for this portfolio. Although the Masons are in the latter part of their investment life cycle, which normally suggests a shorter-than-average time horizon, they have adequate resources available and the expectation of significantly more on an annual basis from the royalty stream. Adopting a longer time horizon will allow them to diversify more effectively and to fund some of their investment objectives that extend beyond their own life expectancies.

Laws and Regulations: No significant regulatory or legal constraints affect the Masons' portfolio other than the need to act with ordinary prudence.

Taxes: The income on this portfolio, combined with expected royalty income in excess of $100,000 a year, will put the Masons into a high tax bracket. Therefore, the investment policy should seek to minimize the tax consequences.

Unique Preferences and Circumstances: The Masons expect to receive substantial income from the royalty agreement. The amount and timing is variable, although the initial estimates are that the income will amount to more than twice Dr. Mason's university salary. Clearly, the realization of royalty income will have an important effect on the income requirements from the portfolio. Although the portfolio should be prepared to pick up the slack should the royalty income stop, the production of above-average current income is unnecessary.

Asset Allocation

Dr. Mason is planning to retire and use investment income from the portfolio, supplemented by income from royalties, to cover living expenses. Because the level of royalty income in the first several years is uncertain, the portfolio initially should be structured to provide for the Masons' entire income requirements. At a minimum, investment income should replace Dr. Mason's salary. After the first several years, assuming that royalties materialize, the portfolio should adopt a growth orientation, with sufficient liquidity to provide for emergency needs should the royalty income slacken or stop suddenly. Although the Masons are late in their life cycle, they do not need to rely solely on the income from their portfolio to support their lifestyle. Thus, the portfolio does not need a pronounced income orientation, and it can reflect a fairly long time horizon.

The asset allocation decision should consider the expected returns from the different asset classes, given the firm's economic outlook and capital market forecast. Specifically, the data indicate that the expected return on stocks is 13.6 percent, compared with historical returns of 10.3 percent; the expected return on Treasury bonds is 11.4 percent, compared with historical returns of 6.4 percent; and the expected return on Treasury bills is 9.4 percent, compared with historical returns of 6.3 percent. Stocks are expected to yield 4.3 percent; bonds, 12.4 percent; and Treasury bills, 9.8 percent. Stocks are clearly attractive, but so are bonds and Treasury bills, and income levels on the latter are extremely high relative to historical levels, whereas income yields on stocks are only average. The Masons' high tax bracket and the need to protect capital suggests the inclusion of high-grade, tax-exempt bonds, if the yields are sufficiently attractive.

In the first year or so, the portfolio should have some liquidity until the Masons' royalty flows are known. An appropriate asset mix would be 50 to 70 percent of the portfolio in stocks, 30 to 40 percent in tax-exempt bonds, and up to 10 percent in tax-exempt cash equivalents. Once the level of royalty income is known, the allocation to cash equivalents can be shifted to stocks or bonds, or both. The Masons will have little need for portfolio liquidity once the royalty income stream begins. This transition portfolio is flexible, and it provides sufficient income in the first year to meet the Masons' return requirements. Assuming a 50 percent stock/30 percent bond/20 percent cash equivalent allocation in the first year, the portfolio will generate about $78,000 in income, a large part of which will be tax-exempt.

The long-run asset allocation should range between 50 and 70 percent stocks, with the balance in bonds; the precise allocation will depend on the level of royalty income generated. If the income stream from the royalty is sufficient to meet the Masons' income objectives, then the portfolio should have a growth orientation. If the royalty does not materialize, the portfolio should have an income orientation. Obviously, a wide middle ground is possible, in which the royalty materializes but falls short of supplying all the Masons' income needs; in this case, the portfolio must balance income and growth appropriately. To meet the Masons' risk objective, the portfolio should be well diversified within the asset classes and contain only high-quality securities. Depending on the portfolio's stock/bond mix, the expected return on the long-run portfolio would range from 12.5 percent (50/50 mix) to 12.9 percent (70/30 mix). The expected yield on the portfolio would fall between 8.4 percent (50/50 mix) and 6.7 percent (70/30 mix).

Although the expected return to stocks and bonds varies considerably across the economic scenarios, time mitigates the risk in these assets, making the volatility of the portfolio acceptable for the Masons. Bonds compose almost half of the portfolio because of their acceptable return and risk as compared to stocks. The data in Exhibit 3 show that stocks offer an incremental expected return of 2.2 percent over bonds, but they do so at a higher level of risk (standard deviation of 16 percent as opposed to 11 percent). The low historic correlation of bonds to stocks indicates that inclusion of both assets would diversify and lower total risk.

The Mason Family (B)

Mr. Mason receives $25,000 a year in retirement income and about $135,000 from the portfolio, a good part of which is tax-exempt. He has stated his desire to give the $200,000 royalty stream to the Essex Institute. He would appear to have more than enough income to live very comfortably, including the payment of any medical bills and the funding of his grandchildren's education. Even though he is in the latter part of his life cycle, current income production is not the predominant return requirement; growth of capital is increasing in importance as he ages.

Revised Investment Policy Statement

Objectives
Return Requirements: Because additional income is of little importance to Mr. Mason, the return objectives are to protect the portfolio from inflation and to provide adequate funds for the education of the grandchildren. The royalty stream is adequate to fund the scholarship.

Risk Tolerance: Because Mr. Mason has no apparent need for additional income, he can afford to increase the volatility of the portfolio so that his family and designated charities will receive a higher expected return.

Constraints
Liquidity: Because income from the portfolio is adequate and his capital needs are inconsequential, liquidity is not an important consideration for Mr. Mason. Further, liquidity is not a necessity for his estate.

Time Horizon: Mr. Mason's shorter-than-average personal time horizon is not of particular significance, because so much of his wealth will go to charity or to his grandchildren, who have much longer time horizons for investment purposes. This longer horizon is the governing consideration in this case.

Laws and Regulations: No change.

Taxes: Mr. Mason is in a high tax bracket and in all likelihood would continue to seek the tax-advantaged investments that are appropriate to his age and circumstances.

Unique Preferences and Circumstances: All major considerations here have been addressed.

Asset Allocation Revisions

The portfolio is currently 70 percent in stocks and 30 percent in bonds. The facts in the case provide no reason to change the allocation, although Water may choose to substitute some international and growth-oriented stocks for the blue-chip stocks to improve the diversification of the portfolio.

Mr. Mason's eventual income of about $185,000 ($25,000 in retirement income and $160,000 in portfolio income) appears more than adequate to meet his stated income requirements. In fact, it is about double the level of income the Masons enjoyed only several years earlier. His willingness to donate the royalty stream to the Essex Institute supports the fact that he has sufficient income. The risk level of the portfolio need not be changed either. In fact, Mr. Mason can spend some of his principal if he needs additional funds. Finally, no significant changes in the constraints merit a change in the allocation of the portfolio.

Because Mr. Mason's income needs are well taken care of, his main priority is to increase the total value of his portfolio for the benefit of his children, grandchildren, and the Essex Institute (should he elect to make an additional bequest in his will). The current mix is accomplishing this goal.

The Allen Family (A)

This case illustrates the resolution of income beneficiary/remainder man interests in a multi-interest trust. It also deals with planning the portfolio of an individual in the light of his residual interest in a trust. Emily Allen, a widow, is the sole income beneficiary of the Allen trust. Her life expectancy is only a few years, and upon her death, her son, George, will inherit the assets of the trust. George does not work but receives—and says he needs—an annual after-tax income of $100,000. This is derived from investment income, supplemented by occasional gifts from his mother. Bowles is to create investment policies and suggest new asset allocations for each Allen portfolio.

Investment Policy: The Trust

Investment policy for the Allen trust must express the investment objectives and consider all relevant constraints on the achievement of the portfolio objectives. In this case, the trust has two sets of interests to satisfy: those of Mrs. Allen, who presently receives all of the income, and George Allen, who will inherit the residual assets free and clear at Mrs. Allen's death. The investment of the trust assets must consider the interests of both. Because the trust assets provide more than sufficient income to meet Mrs. Allen's needs, the primary portfolio objective is inflation-adjusted capital preservation and growth over time.

Objectives

Return Requirements: The primary return objective is inflation-adjusted capital preservation, with a growth-oriented mix to reflect the family entity's need for capital growth over time. Mrs. Allen has sufficient current income, so an income orientation is unnecessary. It would also fail to recognize the remainderman's interests.

Risk Tolerance: The trust can afford moderate to above-average volatility to achieve long-term capital appreciation, as long as Mrs. Allen's income needs are fully met.

Constraints

Liquidity: No immediate liquidity constraints affect the portfolio.

Time Horizon: The time horizon is very long. The trust has more than enough assets to meet income objectives; therefore, the longer term investment objectives—those of future generations—dominate.

Laws and Regulations: Investment of personal trust assets must adhere to appropriate legal and regulatory guidelines. The most relevant one here is that the trust assets must be invested to meet Prudent Man standards on an asset-by-asset basis.

Taxes: The trust income is taxable at high-bracket rates. Therefore, the investment policy must seek to minimize the tax consequences for the Allen family.

Unique Preferences and Circumstances: Nothing about the trust itself is unique. The assets do not belong to Emily, of course, although they provide her with a more-than-adequate income. The existence of the assets is extremely important to George Allen, who expects to inherit them in the near future. George also has a vested interest in the current return from the trust in that his mother subsidizes him when necessary. Bowles should keep in mind that Mrs. Allen has voiced concern about another economic depression.

Investment Policy: George Allen

The appropriate investment policy for George Allen is not so clear-cut. Because he expects to inherit the assets of the Allen trust in the near future, his principal stated concern with regard to his own portfolio is to maximize income production now. It might be several years, however, before the trust assets reach him, and inflation could quickly reduce the buying power of his income.

Objectives

Return Requirements: The primary return objective is to provide $100,000 annually in after-tax income and to do so in a capital-preservation context.

Risk Tolerance: George's aggressive talk is not consistent with the need for his portfolio to be below average in volatility. To meet his current return objective, George must be heavily invested in fixed-income securities; these have little long-run appreciation potential, however. To maintain his standard of living, George can ill afford large fluctuations in the income stream, although he can afford some fluctuations in the value of the portfolio. George's personal risk is relatively low—and his risk tolerance relatively high—because the entire estate will come to him eventuallly. Furthermore, his mother is willing to give him money when he needs it, although he wants to minimize his dependence on these gifts.

Constraints

Liquidity: As long as Mrs. Allen is willing to give George money, he has little need for liquidity in his personal portfolio. Prudence would dictate creating some liquidity for emergencies to avoid a sudden need to sell permanent investments to meet unplanned demands for cash.

Time Horizon: The time horizon may be viewed from two perspectives. Based on George's age, it is probably 30 to 40 years. The current investment policy will change significantly, however, when he inherits the assets of the trust. In that context, the life of the current portfolio is probably very short; investment planning for George could well take place in a series of three-year cycles.

Laws and Regulations: No special legal or regulatory considerations affect the portfolio, except that Bowles must act in a prudent manner.

Taxes: Although George Allen probably generates a fairly large amount of deductions, the size of the income stream means a high tax bracket. The investment policy must seek to minimize the consequences.

Unique Preferences and Circumstances: George Allen's investment perspective is not consistent with his financial muscle or his return objectives, and he should be educated away from his inappropriate approach. To meet his return objective, the portfolio will be heavily invested in fixed-income securities with little appreciation potential. Typically, this allocation would not be prudent for someone of his age. Luckily for George, his mother would probably cover any temporary shortfalls, and he enjoys the prospect of inheriting the trust, probably within a few years.

Capital Market Outlook

Perennial Trust's forecasts and scenario data (Exhibit 3) generate the following expected values:

	Expected Annual Total Return	*Expected Annual Yield*
Cash equivalents	5.2%	5.2%
Common stocks	10.6	3.8
Domestic bonds	14.0	12.8
Tax-exempt bonds	7.6	6.8
Equity real estate	7.6	9.0

Assuming a 40 percent tax rate, the after-tax expected yield on cash equivalents is 3.1 percent, on stocks is 2.3 percent, on real estate is 5.4 percent, on tax-exempt bonds is 6.8 percent, and on domestic bonds is 7.7 percent.

Asset Allocation

To meet the capital preservation objective, the Allen trust's assets should be skewed toward stocks and real estate, although the portfolio should continue to include a meaningful holding of bonds. Income production will continue to be completely adequate, and annual fluctuations in asset value are of no real concern to Mrs. Allen. The projected returns on tax-exempt bonds are competitive, so they should compose the bond allocation. Because the trust requires few reserves, it does not need to include more than a working balance of cash equivalents.

The suggested mix for the Allen trust is 50 to 60 percent in stocks, 10 to 20 percent in real estate, and the balance in tax-exempt bonds. The recommended portfolio is 55 percent in stocks, 30 percent in tax-exempt bonds, and 15 percent in real estate.

This portfolio would yield 4.1 percent after taxes and generate almost $640,000 annually in after-tax income. The high allocation to stocks and bonds provides for inflation adjustment of the assets and income stream. The bonds provide some diversification and risk reduction, that is, they lower the volatility of the portfolio. Because liquidity is unimportant, nothing is allocated to cash equivalents. The fixed-income portion of the portfolio should be tax-free bonds as long as the after-tax yields are competitive with the yields on Treasury bonds.

At some point, Bowles may wish to suggest an even broader diversification in the portfolio, including venture capital and international equity investments for inflation-hedging purposes. The Allen trust's assets are sufficient to support such breadth, and George Allen would probably endorse it.

George Allen

George Allen's income requirement limits the flexibility of the asset allocation for his own portfolio. Assuming the venture capital is relatively illiquid and the real estate cannot be sold because it is owned with the trust, George's portfolio will need to be invested 70 percent in tax-free bonds to meet his stated income goal of $100,000. The following allocation would satisfy his income needs:

	After-Tax Yield	Allocation $	Allocation %	After-Tax Annual Income
Bonds (tax-exempt)	6.8%	$1,250,000	70%	$ 85,000
Real Estate	5.4	300,000	17	16,200
Growth stocks	1.0	150,000	8	1,250
Venture Capital	0.0	100,000	5	0
		$1,800,000	100%	$102,450

This portfolio has little growth potential. The allocation of 8 percent to growth stocks, which yield only 1 percent as compared with 2.3 percent for the S&P 500, is to provide as much inflation protection as possible within the equity allocation. The venture capital investment could have growth potential, but probably not for several years to come; in the interim, it generates no income. The $100,000 of after-tax income should be fairly stable because its basic component is bonds and the yield is not expected to change significantly across the different scenarios. George is subject to substantial purchasing-power risk, call risk, and reinvestment risk, however. Furthermore, the income-oriented portfolio is unlikely to increase his capital. In fact, it is not likely to preserve the real value of the assets.

Bowles must advise George of the risks associated with a heavy allocation to bonds. The allocation to bonds is justified, in part, because George stands to inherit substantial assets in the not-too-distant future and because his mother is willing to give him financial assistance meanwhile. The inheritance will provide adequate assets to support him for the rest of his life, so his current portfolio can be structured to provide only income for the next few years.

The Allen Family (B)

This case provides an opportunity to untangle the conflicting investment objectives of George Allen. He can no longer afford to keep his portfolio invested 70 percent in bonds if he wishes to maintain his lifestyle in years to come.

George must be advised of the risks associated with his portfolio. If he insists that he needs $100,000 a year in after-tax income, his portfolio will remain heavily invested in bonds. This leaves him open to inflation risk, call risk, and reinvestment risk. If Mrs. Allen lives 20 years, George's life style will be severely constrained. To invest in assets more oriented toward growth, however, he would have to accept a reduced lifestyle or get a job now, or both.

The Allen Trust

Nothing in this case calls for revision of the investment policy or reallocation of the trust assets. The primary return objective remains to provide for inflation-adjusted capital preservation, to be achieved at moderate to above-average risk. The major difference is that Mrs. Allen is now expected to spend her income on herself, her grandchildren's education, medical research, and charity; she no longer plans to make gifts to her son, George. Mrs. Allen receives in excess of $600,000 in after-tax income from the trust. This should be sufficient to meet her own living expenses and to make the $250,000 annual contribution to charity. If a shortfall threatens, the portfolio allocation could be shifted toward greater income production. The present structure of the portfolio also protects the assets against inflation.

George Allen

The investment policy and asset allocation for George Allen will need revision. In addition, Bowles must advise George that he will have to accept a lower standard of living or go back to work. Mrs. Allen has declared her intention not to support George financially. Therefore, George's portfolio will have to be invested as if he will not receive any additional cash from his mother for the next 10 to 20 years.

A revised investment policy for George Allen is:

Objectives
Return Requirements: The returns should be sufficient to provide George with a realistic level of inflation-adjusted income to meet his basic living expenses.
Risk Tolerance: A higher-than-average level of volatility will be necessary to afford some inflation protection.

Constraints

Liquidity: The portfolio should provide some liquidity because George has no other source of capital.

Time Horizon: The shortest planning time horizon is equal to Mrs. Allen's life expectancy, now 10 to 20 years.

Laws and Regulations: No special legal or regulatory constraints of importance apply here.

Taxes: The income level places George in a high tax bracket. Investment policy should seek to minimize the tax consequences.

Unique Preferences and Circumstances: George must now rely solely on the income from this portfolio, unless he gets a job, because his mother has stated she does not intend to support him. Unfortunately, the portfolio is unlikely to satisfy his desire for a $100,000 after-tax real annual income level over a 10- to 20-year investment horizon. George will need to accept either a steadily declining real income or a more growth-oriented allocation with a lower income level but some prospect of an increase over time.

Based on the revised investment policy statement, a reasonable asset mix for George's portfolio would be a balanced mix of bonds and growth stocks. The choice between taxable and tax-exempt bonds should reflect their relative after-tax returns. In this case, the tax-exempt bonds provide competitive expected yields. Assuming that the real estate investment is still attractive, it should be kept because it is expected to yield more than 5 percent and offers some inflation protection. Furthermore, it is owned in the trust. Thus, the recommended allocation is as follows:

	After-Tax Yield	Allocation $	Allocation %	After-Tax Annual Income
Cash equivalents	3.1%	$ 50,000	3%	$ 1,550
Bonds (tax-exempt)	6.8	725,000	40	49,300
Growth stocks	1.0	725,000	40	7,250
Real estate	5.4	300,000	17	16,200
		$1,800,000	100%	$74,300

This structure will generate an expected annual income of $74,300 and will provide better inflation protection than did the previous allocation. The recommended allocation does not meet George Allen's income objective, but Bowles has an educational role to play, and facts are facts. The choice of income level is George's; once Bowles shows him what is reasonable, prudent, and the best bet for the future, George's choice will dictate what management Bowles will provide. Once the choice is made, a new investment policy statement and asset mix may be required.

The Ramez Family (A)

This case introduces several aspects of international investing for individuals by bringing international equities, real estate, and precious metals into the individual investor complex. The Ramez family, recent emigrants to the United States, have realized $10 million from the sale of their business in the Philippines. After a few years, Luis Ramez intends to return to business, using a portion of his $10 million to fund it. His wife wishes to pursue charitable activities. The three Ramez children are presently living overseas and from time to time receive financial assistance from their parents. Lius Ramez is particularly apprehensive about economic devastation in the form of drastic inflation or depression.

Investment Policy Statement

The investment policy should reflect the return and risk objectives of the Ramez family, as well as all relevant constraints on achieving those objectives.

Objectives

Return Requirements: The two return objectives are to provide for family income needs of $400,000 a year after taxes (roughly a 4 percent net yield requirement) and to maintain the purchasing power of the Ramez family wealth over time.

Risk Tolerance. The Ramez family's biggest concern is protecting the portfolio from the ravages of extreme economic environments such as deflation/depression and rampant inflation. Therefore, Lindell should try to structure the portfolio so as to achieve above-average total portfolio flexibility and adequate liquidity. This goal can be accomplished with moderate risk taking accompanied by diversification across a broad array of assets.

Constraints

Time Horizon: The time horizon should be viewed in two stages. The first might be two or three years, during which Mr. Ramez may require capital to start another business. In the second stage, the time horizon is longer, with the Ramez family investing for their own needs, for future generations, and possibly for charities in the Philippines.

Liquidity: Mr. Ramez's desire to be able to raise cash on short notice implies more-than-normal liquidity and special attention to asset marketability. Over time, a sizable amount of liquidity could be needed to meet the demands of (1) Mr. Ramez's renewed interest in business, (2) problems the children might encounter, and (3) special charitable contributions.

Laws and Regulations: No special legal or regulatory problems seem to exist, although transferring funds to the children might pose some technical and tax problems.

Taxes: Mr. Ramez expects to pay taxes like any other U.S. citizen. He has not asked Dexter for tax advice.

Unique Preferences and Circumstances: Special considerations are important here. The Ramez family is scattered throughout the world. If the Ramez parents plan to send their children money overseas, then some international exposure in the portfolio might be advisable in order to hedge against exchange rate fluctuations. Mr. Ramez has experienced the ravages of both inflation and depression in his native Philippines and has expressed a desire that the portfolio maintain its purchasing power in the worst of economic times. Hence, the portfolio should be broadly diversified, with some assets that do well in an inflationary environment and some that do well in a deflationary environment. He also has requested a 5 percent allocation to precious metals.

Asset Allocation

An asset allocation that emphasizes equities accomplishes the objectives fairly well. The portfolio should have 50 to 70 percent in equities, 15 to 25 percent in bonds, 5 to 10 percent in Treasury bills, 5 to 10 percent in real estate, and 5 percent in precious metals. Quality and marketability should be stressed on all assets.

The expected high income yield and the unusually low incremental expected total return of stocks versus bonds suggests that a higher-than-average allocation to bonds is warranted. Furthermore, the bonds are the best-performing asset class in the deflation scenario.

One portfolio that meets the policy is: domestic stocks (40 percent), international stocks (20 percent), bonds (25 percent), cash equivalents (5 percent), real estate (5 percent), and—as requested—precious metals (5 percent). This allocation provides adequate liquidity, meets the stated income objective, and most importantly, provides broad diversification.

Based on the recommended allocation, the portfolio produces the following results:

	Total Annual Return	*After-tax Annual Yield*
Low inflation	11.6%	4.2%
Inflation	5.6	6.0
Deflation	-3.5	2.3
Expected value	7.4	4.2

The portfolio hedges the inflation and deflation scenarios reasonably well. Liquidity is maintained, a reasonable level of international exposure exists, and the downside protection is reasonably good.

Manager Selection

The three international portfolio managers have different styles and performance records. None of the managers outperformed the EAFE Index, although all of them outperformed the S&P 500. Their volatility and the proportion of currency exposure differ.

Manager A has the lowest average return (20.4 percent) and the lowest volatility, measured by standard deviation. Manager A's performance is highly correlated with the performance of the S&P 500, although this may be merely coincidental, because Manager A has a large average currency exposure.

Manager B has the highest average return (28.2 percent) and the highest volatility of all three managers. Manager B's performance is highly correlated with that of the EAFE Index but is higher in volatility.

Manager C has the second highest average return (28 percent), although this performance is insignificantly different from the performance of Manager B. Manager C had significantly lower volatility than Manager B, however. Manager C relied more heavily on currency swings favoring the dollar than did Manager B.

Selection of managers is largely a subjective exercise, with "chemistry" playing an important role. The information provided is insufficient to document the quantitative superiority of any of these managers relative to the others. Therefore, Lindell will have to determine which manager best matches the Ramezes' attitudes toward investment management. Other things being equal, Lindell should seek competence in managing in non-U.S. markets. Comparisons to S&P performance are not really germane here.

The Ramez Family (B)

This case provides an opportunity to revise an investment policy and asset allocation in a situation in which nearly half of the portfolio assets are being withdrawn from the portfolio and invested in a hard-to-value investment alternative.

Investment Policy Statement

To reflect recent developments, the Ramez investment policy should be revised as follows:

Objectives

Return Requirements: The investment goal shifts from the production of income to appreciation in the Dexter-managed residual portfolio. The royalty income should be sufficient, even after taxes, to meet the $425,000 annual income requirement and to return the investment in 10 years.

Risk Tolerance: The Ramez family's tolerance for risk (volatility) has increased in that one important call on liquidity has been met. The royalty represents a significant business risk, however, and the balance of the portfolio should avoid duplicating that specific risk.

Constraints

Liquidity: The large cash flow reduces liquidity needs, but the illiquidity of the new investment suggests that other assets should remain marketable in case conversion of a further portion of the portfolio to cash is required.

Time Horizon: This remains a two-level consideration, but with different dimensions than before. The first horizon is now 1 to 10 years, and the second, from 25 years (the Ramezes' life expectancy) to infinity (future generations).

Laws and Regulations: No change.

Taxes: Taxes remain an important consideration; in particular, the effect of taxes on royalty income must be determined and minimized if possible.

Unique Preferences and Circumstances: The reinvestment problem of the royalty cash flow must be addressed. Also, the existence of this sizable asset in its unique form will alter commitments in other components of the portfolio.

Portfolio Restructuring

The portfolio should be restructured so that income is completely deemphasized in favor of growth. The royalty is equivalent to an annuity (fixed-income asset substitute) with a specified life. The cash flow, after meeting income needs, must be invested so as to recoup the inflation-adjusted principal in 10 years. Because the investment is so large and involves a natural resource, precious metals should be eliminated from the portfolio, as should any energy or other raw materials stocks. Close attention should be paid to potential dividend growth so that income production in the 10th year and beyond will meet the stated requirements.

The royalty's fixed-income qualities eliminate the need for domestic and international bonds in the portfolio. The royalty's commodity base contributes inflation protection, making real estate an unnecessary, though still acceptable, asset; the illiquidity of physical real estate argues against that form, however.

The revised portfolio should be invested in equities, with a small (less than 5 percent) cash position for liquidity. Within equities, 60 to 70 percent should be invested in domestic equities, with the balance in international equities. This portfolio meets the growth-orientation objective. The royalty income and dividend income meet the income objective.

The royalty investment will generate more cash than the Ramez family needs in a year. This extra cash flow, some of which is really a return of principal, must be reinvested. Assuming a 2 percent dividend yield on the stocks, the Ramez portfolio will generate an estimated $140,000 a year in income, or 33 percent of the family's income requirement. The royalty will provide the additional $285,000 a year. Thus, the royalty income in excess of $285,000 should be reinvested. An argument could be made for investing the excess in long-term bonds to replace the royalty as it declines and to diversify the portfolio.

Ednam Products

This case deals with defined-contribution profit-sharing plans. It describes the personal circumstances of four Ednam Products employees who will be choosing their investments in the vehicles provided in Ednam's new defined-contribution plan. An important point about such plans is that individual investment choices will differ depending on the circumstances, age, and risk aversion of each participant. The opportunity to rebalance a defined-contribution portfolio will make each person a potential market timer. Trotter, the company's Assistant Treasurer, must encourage each employee to take a long-term perspective and make an appropriate basic asset allocation. The portfolios should be rebalanced only to the extent that an employee's objectives, risk aversion, or basic circumstances change.

Margaret Custer

The investment policy for Margaret Custer should reflect her youth and apparent capacity to assume an aggressive risk posture.

Objectives

Return Requirement: With a long time horizon and a wealth-building posture, the objective is to maximize total return.

Risk Tolerance: Custer can afford an above-average risk level. The plan will be building for many years; therefore, interim volatility of assets is not a major consideration.

Constraints

Liquidity: No liquidity constraints apply, given Custer's youth and the assumption that the assets cannot be touched.

Time Horizon: The time horizon is very long, at least 30 years until Custer's retirement and then an additional 10 to 20 years of life expectancy.

Laws and Regulations: This investment has no particular legal consequences, although it must comply with whatever rules the company has set up to govern participation in the profit-sharing plan, and plan administration must reflect ERISA qualification standards.

Taxes: Returns can compound tax-free in the profit-sharing plan account.

Unique Preferences and Circumstances: Custer, in buying a $70,000 condominium, is providing an outside real estate equity investment.

With a focus on long time horizon and an aggressive posture with respect to risk, an appropriate allocation is

Domestic stock fund	40%
Small-capitalization fund	20
International stock fund	20
Real estate fund	10
Bond fund	10

This portfolio is 80 percent in equity funds, 10 percent in real estate, and 10 percent in the bond fund. The combination of stock funds provides broad diversification across the equity asset class; the real estate fund, supplementing Custer's outside condo holding, is primarily for exposure of a different equity type and for diversification. The 10 percent in bonds also provides some diversification. There is no need for liquidity in the plan account at this time.

Glenn Abbott

Although Glenn Abbott is 12 years older than Margaret Custer, he is still at least 20 years from retirement. His objectives and constraints are not significantly different from Custer's, so his investment policy and asset allocation should be similar to hers.

Objectives

Return Requirement: With a long time horizon and an aggressive risk posture, the objective is to maximize total return.

Risk Tolerance: Abbott can afford an above-average risk posture. The plan will be building for many years, therefore volatility of asset values is not a major consideration here. Abbott's risk tolerance may decrease in three to four years if he plans to borrow against the assets in his retirement plan to fund his children's college education.

Constraints

Liquidity: Liquidity constraints are not present, given Abbott's relative youth and the assumption that plan assets cannot be touched.

Time Horizon: The time horizon is long, at least 20 years to retirement and then an additional 10 to 20 years of life expectancy.

Laws and Regulations: This investment has no particular legal consequences, although it must comply with whatever rules the company has set up to govern participation in the profit-sharing plan.

Taxes: Returns can compound tax-free in the profit-sharing plan account.

Unique Preferences and Circumstances: Abbott is buying a $100,000 house, with a $75,000 mortgage. He has a $25,000 savings account. He has two children approaching college age.

Glenn, like Margaret, has a long time horizon and can be relatively aggressive from a risk standpoint. Thus, an appropriate allocation is

Domestic stock fund	35%
Small-capitalization fund	15
International stock fund	20
Real estate fund	10
Bond fund	20

This portfolio is 70 percent in stock funds, 10 percent in the real estate fund, and 20 percent in the bond fund. Abbott's allocation is similar to Custer's, but the risk level has been reduced somewhat. Abbott has two children approaching college age. He may need to borrow against the value of his profit-sharing plan for their education. This possibility suggests a higher allocation to bonds to reduce the volatility of the portfolio. The combination of equity funds provides a growth orientation and broad diversification within this asset class. The real estate fund supplements his $25,000 equity position in his house. Liquidity needs are provided by his $25,000 savings account. There is no need for additional liquidity in the plan account at this time.

Tom Davis

Tom Davis plans to retire in four years, but his life expectancy is much longer. The investment policy suggested assumes that Davis can roll his mutual fund investments into his IRA when he leaves the retirement plan.

Objectives

Return Requirement: The return objective is shifting from a total return objective to an income orientation with adequate inflation protection to meet Davis' retirement needs over his life expectancy. Production of current income should be in the tax-sheltered environment of the profit-sharing account or an IRA, not in his personal accounts.

Risk Tolerance: Davis' tolerance for volatility is low to moderate. Although his retirement date is approaching, the time horizon for his portfolio is still relatively long.

Constraints

Liquidity: Liquidity is increasing in importance as Davis approaches retirement. The portfolio allocation will be shifting toward an income orientation as Davis prepares to leave the plan in four years. The presence of some liquidity would be prudent to avoid a sudden need to sell permanent investments to meet unforeseen demands for cash.

Time Horizon: The time horizon is intermediate to long, although the policy should reflect the fact that Davis plans to retire in four years. His life expectancy, however, is 15 to 20 years.

Laws and Regulations: This investment has no particular legal consequences, although it must comply with whatever rules the company has set up to govern participation in the plan.

Taxes: Returns can compound tax-free in the profit-sharing plan account. Davis is most likely in a high tax bracket personally.

Unique Preferences and Circumstances: Davis must begin the transition from building his retirement assets to establishing an inflation-protected income stream for his retirement. He should consider his nonplan assets as well, because in four years they will be merged with his plan assets to provide for his retirement needs. Davis has $50,000 in an IRA, $50,000 in a money market account, a $100,000 portfolio of growth stocks, and $135,000 of equity in his home.

With a focus on an intermediate-term time horizon and a low-to-moderate tolerance for risk, the portfolio should be balanced to reduce volatility. Excluding the equity in his personal residence, the allocation for the next four years could be 50 to 60 percent in equities, 30 to 40 percent in bonds, and 10 to 20 percent in cash reserves.
Excluding his residence, Davis' nonplan asset allocation is

Growth stocks	$100,000	50%
Small-capitalization stocks (IRA)	50,000	25
Money market account	50,000	25
	$200,000	100%

According to his investment policy, the allocation should be shifted away from growth stocks and towards an income orientation with lower volatility. To reduce the growth emphasis now present, the small-capitalization stocks in Davis' IRA should be switched to a high-quality bond fund. This can take place tax-free within the IRA if gains are realized, and the much higher income can compound tax-free.
An appropriate allocation, excluding his residence, is:

Retirement plan:		
Domestic stock fund	$ 80,000	22%
Bond fund	80,000	22
	$160,000	44%
Nonplan financial assets:		
Growth-oriented stock portfolio	$100,000	28%
Bond fund (IRA)	50,000	14
Cash reserves	50,000	14
	$200,000	56%
Combined assets:	$360,000	100%

Summarized by asset class, the combined portfolio is 50 percent stocks, 36 percent bonds, and 14 percent cash equivalents. When the real estate equity is included, the total assets equal $495,000 and the allocation is 37 percent stocks, 26 percent bonds, 27 percent real estate equity, and 10 percent cash equivalents. This allocation represents a good balance between growth needs and income production while providing inflation protection, liquidity, and effective use of the IRA and retirement plan account tax shelters.

Pete Jones

Jones is very near retirement. Investment of his plan assets must be done with full consideration of his outside assets in order to maximize their value relative to his needs and goals. Investment policy will reflect this requirement and assume that Jones can roll his retirement plan account mutual fund investments into his IRA when he leaves the retirement plan.

Objectives

Return Requirement: The portfolio must now reflect Jones' post-retirement objectives. The return objective is to provide Jones with sufficient income in retirement, on an inflation-adjusted basis, to meet his needs. Production of current income should be in the tax-sheltered environment of the profit-sharing account or IRA, not in Jones' personal accounts.

Risk Tolerance: Jones' capacity for risk is below average. In retirement, he will not be able to tolerate large fluctuations in the income stream. At the same time, inflation protection will also be important and some risk will have to be accepted to obtain it.

Constraints

Liquidity: Liquidity is increasing in importance as Jones approaches retirement. The presence of some liquidity would be prudent to avoid a sudden need to sell permanent investments to meet unforeseen demands for cash.

Time Horizon: The time horizon is shorter than average for a defined contribution participant, although it should cover Jones' life expectancy, or 10 to 20 years.

Laws and Regulations: This investment has no particular legal consequences, although it must comply with whatever rules the company has set up to govern participation in the plan.

Taxes: The income from the retirement plan is taxable as Jones withdraws it from the plan. After age 70½, he must begin to withdraw the funds according to the Internal Revenue Service formula.

Unique Preferences and Circumstances: Jones must make the transition from building his retirement assets to establishing an inflation-protected income stream for retirement. Jones' investment policy and asset allocation should incorporate the $150,000 equity in his house, the $100,000 IRA, the $125,000 portfolio of blue-chip stocks, and the $100,000 in savings.

With a focus on a 10- to 20-year time horizon and a low-to-moderate tolerance for risk, the portfolio should be balanced to reduce volatility and promote inflation protection. Excluding the equity real estate, an appropriate allocation is 45 to 55 percent in stocks, 35 to 45 percent in bonds, and 10 to 20 percent in cash reserves.

Excluding his residence, Jones's nonplan asset allocation is

Blue-Chip stocks	$125,000	38%
Bond fund (IRA)	100,000	31
Bank CDs	100,000	31
	$325,000	100%

Given his circumstances and likely needs and goals, the allocation should be shifted toward an income orientation with lower volatility and more effective use of cash. An appropriate allocation, excluding the equity in his residence, is

Retirement plan:		
Domestic stock fund	$105,000	19%
Bond fund	120,000	22
	$225,000	41%
Nonplan financial assets:		
Blue-Chip Stocks	$170,000	31%
Bond fund (IRA)	100,000	18
Cash reserves	55,000	10
	$325,000	59%
Combined assets:	$550,000	100%

Summarized by asset class, the portfolio is 50 percent stocks, 40 percent bonds, and 10 percent cash equivalents. This allocation involves investing 45 percent of the money currently in bank CDs in stocks. This decision should have no adverse tax consequences.

When the equity in Jones' personal residence is included, the total assets equal $700,000 and the allocation is 40 percent stocks, 31 percent bonds, 21 percent equity real estate, and 8 percent cash equivalents. This portfolio will provide approximately $34,000 in income annually, as well as good balance and reasonable inflation protection.

Mid-South Trucking Company

Investing for defined-contribution plans is quite different from investing for defined-benefit plans. This case introduces the key features of defined-benefit retirement plans. The president of a trucking firm asks an outside advisor to explain how the two types of retirement plans differ and how the retirement fund portfolio's asset allocation might vary depending on which format the firm adopts.

Investment Policy
An appropriate investment policy statement for the Mid-South defined-benefit pension plan would be:

Objectives
Return Requirements: The portfolio should achieve an inflation-protected rate of return at least equal to the actuarial assumption of 7 percent. Returns in excess of 7 percent may be used to reduce company contributions or increase employee benefits.

Risk Tolerance: The company on balance has the flexibility to accept an average to above-average degree of risk. Key factors to consider in reaching conclusions regarding risk tolerance are:

- The defined-benefit plan must meet ERISA prudence requirements, which apply to the entire portfolio, not just its individual component securities.
- Mid-South's two key actuarial assumptions with regard to return and salary progression are relatively conservative. The rate of return assumption of 7 percent is reasonable relative to historic results of 10 percent and to present expectations. A salary progression rate of 5 percent is about "normal" and in line with past results.
- The plan is valued on a four-year rolling average. This is a relatively conservative approach that smooths market fluctuations.
- Mid-South's average employee age is reasonably low, and the time horizon long.
- Mid-South's operating results have not been particularly cyclical.
- One aspect of the plan would act to moderate risk taking and suggest a more conservative approach. Past service liabilities are relatively high and are to be amortized over a 35-year period of time. This is a liberal approach toward funding past service liabilities.

Constraints

Liquidity: The company's liquidity requirements are about average. Income must be sufficient to meet payments to retirees, but contributions are available for continuing investment.

Time Horizon: The company's time horizon is relatively long (longer than the normal market cycle) because the company has young employees and no short-term liquidity needs.

Laws and Regulations: Regulatory and legal considerations are relatively minor. Under ERISA provisions, the Prudent Expert rule applies to the total portfolio, the plan cannot hold more than 10 percent of its own stock, and the portfolio must be diversified and managed for the sole benefit of plan participants.

Taxes: Tax considerations are not a meaningful constraint in this case. The plan is tax-exempt.

Unique Preferences and Circumstances: The plan's present 100 percent bond orientation is unique and a matter of concern, given ERISA's diversification demands. Mr. Oliver wants the plan to serve as an actively managed profit center that will maximize return for a given level of risk. This request is not all that unique, but the portfolio must be constructed carefully in respect of ERISA's "sole benefit of the participants" rule.

Asset Allocation

The appropriate asset allocation will depend on the return expectation for the asset classes and the plan's objectives and constraints. Based on Exhibit 2, the probability-weighted return expectations are currently as follows:

Cash equivalents	6.40%
Domestic stocks (S&P 500 Index)	10.05
Domestic bonds	7.35

These return expectations and the plan's objectives and constraints indicate a relatively aggressive asset-allocation strategy is appropriate. The following ranges could be adopted as the long-term norms:

Cash equivalents	0-5%
Domestic stocks	50-75
Domestic bonds	20-50

The plan's limited liquidity requirements permit a low level of short-term reserves, which in any event currently do not meet the plan's 7 percent return requirement. All of the constraints except the past service liability aspect suggest that moderate emphasis on common stocks is appropriate. An average to below-average bond position is indicated. Ten-year bonds might be favored initially because they provide some price stability and a yield 1.5 percentage points higher than the 7 percent return requirement.

General Technology (A)

In this case, the company elects to unbundle its retirement plan's assets and withdraw from the all-annuity format in favor of separate pension and profit-sharing portfolios. The case illustrates the key considerations involved in investing for a defined-benefit pension plan. The task is to contrast the expected performance of different asset classes in various economic environments and to choose the most appropriate investment policy and asset allocation for the pension fund. The issues raised for the firm's defined-contribution profit-sharing plan are addressed in the related case, Profit-Sharing Advisory, Inc.

Investment Policy Statement

The investment policy for the defined-benefit pension plan must fully reflect the objectives of the plan and all relevant constraints and preferences.

Objectives

Return Requirements: The return objective should emphasize total return, including both capital appreciation and current income, in a long-term, inflation-protected context. Because little immediate need exists for current cash flows as a contribution supplement and because the benefit obligations are long-term in nature, the policy should favor flexibility and avoid overemphasis on current income production.

Risk Tolerance: The plan can tolerate above-normal volatility in investment returns given its long time horizon, the existence of a profit-sharing supplement to the pension benefit, and the absence of unusual circumstances.

Constraints

Liquidity: With the expected normal level of company contributions, the pension fund has no unusual liquidity needs, and nothing in the case suggests that this will change in the early future.

Time Horizon: The time horizon for this pension fund is long. The company is a relatively young, successful, and growing firm. Although the case is not specific, one could assume that the workforce is also relatively young. The presence of an older, more mature workforce would shorten the horizon, but it would still be long term.

Laws and Regulations: As a corporate retirement plan, this plan's operation is subject to ERISA provisions. Basically, the Act requires plan management to reflect a Prudent Expert standard.

Taxes: Because the GTC pension plan is tax-exempt, taxes are not a significant investment factor.

Unique Preferences and Circumstances: No unique considerations will affect the portfolio.

Asset Mix Recommendation

A range is recommended, with advisor leeway to alter the actual allocation within the range depending on the economic and capital market outlook. An allocation of 50 to 70 percent stocks, 35 to 50 percent bonds, up to 5 percent cash equivalents, and up to 10 percent real estate would meet the objectives and constraints outlined in the investment policy statement. This range is appropriate because

- It is dominated by stocks and bonds, which are expected to provide the highest returns over the forecast horizon.
- A young company like GTC should be most concerned about inflation protection, which stocks and real estate are more likely to provide over the long run.
- Liquidity is not a major consideration, so the allocation to cash and real estate can be small.
- Despite its mediocre near-term outlook, real estate should be included for its historically high returns and its ability to provide inflation protection and diversification over the long term.

Thus, of the choices, asset Mix 5 is most appropriate for General Technology.

Asset Performance Analysis

Investment Committee View

Based on the Investment Committee's expectation of moderate growth and steady or declining inflation, bonds appear to offer the unusual prospect of slightly higher potential return with significantly less risk than stocks. The Investment Committee also believes these asset classes will generate very high real returns. Real estate appears relatively unattractive under this scenario; the returns are expected to be well below historical levels, and the risk is higher than historical levels. The Investment Committee's view would lead toward a portfolio emphasizing bonds, with a less-than-normal stock position and only a minimal amount of cash equivalents. The Committee expects a negative correlation between stock and bond returns. Under these conditions, the mixture of these two asset classes would result in abnormally low portfolio risk. For this scenario, Mix 6 is recommended.

Return-to-Inflation View

Based on this view, the portfolio should be more heavily weighted toward stocks. Stocks are expected to provide an extremely attractive return at a level of risk slightly higher than historical standards. Because returns from stocks are fairly highly correlated with inflation, they provide a good inflation hedge. Under this scenario, bonds are expected to provide reasonably attractive real returns, despite the negative correlation between bond returns and inflation. Cash looks more attractive under this scenario than under the Investment Committee view, as does real estate (higher return, lower risk). Real estate also has a very high correlation with inflation. Nevertheless, it is expected to be less attractive in the future than it has been in the recent past. The Return-to-Inflation view would lead toward a portfolio that is more than normally weighted toward stocks, with some bonds and Treasury bills for diversification and perhaps a small commitment to real estate. For this scenario, Mix 5 is recommended.

General Technology (B)

The Investment Committee economic scenario is now characterized by a significantly lower inflation rate and real GNP growth rate than before. This view results in a dramatic decline in the expected return for all asset classes. Stocks are now significantly less attractive, and the decline in their expected return is accompanied by an increase in risk. Real estate also has a lower expected return than it did originally and higher expected risk.

Given the new outlook, Mix 3 is now the choice because:

- Stocks are now less attractive because of their lower return and higher risk.
- Although expected bond returns have also declined dramatically, the risk/return trade-off appears more attractive than that for stocks. A synthesis of the Investment Committee view and the Return-to-Inflation view, rather than the Investment Committee's view alone, would have supported a lower bond weighting than would be reflected in Mix 3.
- Real estate is now quite unattractive considering its low expected return and relatively high risk.

Asset Mix 3 is within the allocation ranges recommended in Part A.

Profit-Sharing Advisory, Inc. (A)

This case develops the profit-sharing plan described in General Technology Corporation. In it, the advisor must disentangle an employee's misconceptions about investment and devise an appropriate investment policy and asset allocation.

Investment Policy Statement

Williams' comments about investment indicate that he does not have a clear or consistent understanding of the relationship between risk and return. A more appropriate set of investment objectives and constraints for Williams' profit-sharing account would be:

Objectives

Return Requirements: The primary return objective is to maximize total return and build capital taking maximum advantage of the plan's tax-sheltered aspects.

Risk Tolerance: The risk tolerance would be above-average given the long time horizon and the Williams family's ability to accept more than normal volatility in asset values.

Constraints

Liquidity: Liquidity constraints are not present in the plan given Williams' relative youth and the assumption that plan assets cannot be touched. Existence of a modest savings account, together with Williams' good credit standing and ability to borrow for temporary or emergency needs, suggests minimal liquidity in the plan portfolio.

Time horizon: A relatively long time horizon can be assumed for planning purposes. The assets are likely to remain invested for at least 20 years in the retirement plan, and Williams' life expectancy extends beyond that.

Laws and Regulations: This investment has no particular legal consequences, although it must comply with whatever rules the company has set up to govern participation in the profit-sharing plan. As individual investors, the Williamses have maximum flexibility without legal or regulatory constraint.

Taxes: Returns can compound tax-free in the profit-sharing plan account; the Williamses are in a high tax bracket for income received personally (40 percent currently).

Unique Preferences and Circumstances: The Williamses appear to have no current income pressures—they are net savers now and probably will be for an extended period ahead. Starting in 11 or 12 years, however, their three young children may be following one another into college within a relatively short space of time. The Williamses' investment policy should consider their $10,000 in General Technology stock, $25,000 in bank CDs, $5,000 in cash reserves, and the $40,000 of equity in their home, in addition to Williams' profit-sharing account of $130,000.

Asset Allocation

Williams should be discouraged from managing his investments one year at a time to try to keep pace with changing short-term economic and other considerations. That strategy would increase turnover, reduce returns, and require Williams to rebalance and reallocate his investments more-or-less continuously.

As encompassed in the investment policy statement, building capital is the major task, with no current income pressures but a need to hold the overall risk down. The tax situation dictates that any high-yielding assets be sheltered in the profit-sharing account. Tax-advantaged assets and those oriented toward capital gain should be held in the personal account. The horizon is relatively long and only minimal liquidity need be maintained for emergency purposes.

In counseling the Williamses, Martin should urge them to use initial allocation ranges of 60 to 80 percent equities, 20 to 30 percent bonds, 10 to 15 percent real estate, and 5 percent cash. Given the Williamses' conservative posture, the following mix, which excludes their personal real estate, is recommended:

Profit-sharing assets:		
Common stock fund	$ 42,500	25%
Growth stock fund	34,000	20
Bond fund	36,500	21
Equity real estate	17,000	10
	$130,000	76%
Personal assets:		
Growth stock fund	$ 22,000	13%
Common stock (GTC)	10,000	6
Money market account	8,000	5
	$ 40,000	24%
Combined assets:	$170,000	100%

By asset class, the combined assets would be 64 percent in stocks, 21 percent in bonds, 10 percent in equity real estate, and 5 percent in cash equivalents. Including the Williamses' equity in their residence, the unified mix would be 52 percent in stocks, 27 percent in real estate, 17 percent in bonds, and 4 percent in cash.

The profit-sharing account is 59 percent in equities, 28 percent in bonds, and 13 percent in equity real estate. It is also recommended that Williams invest his personal account assets more aggressively, shifting from 25 percent equities and 75 percent in bank CDs and cash to 80 percent equities and 20 percent in cash. The $8,000 money market account is recommended so that Williams will have some liquidity for emergencies and unforseen events requiring cash.

Profit-Sharing Advisory, Inc. (B)

This case requires modification of the investment policy and asset allocation developed in the first part of the case to account for changed financial circumstances. The Williams family has received a windfall of $50,000 a year for 25 years, which changes their investment perspective considerably, particularly because they do not expect to change their current income needs.

Revised Investment Policy

The objectives of the retirement plan do not change significantly. The primary return objective remains to maximize total return and build capital. The Williams family's need for current income from their investments has been reduced to a minimum. The family's ability (and presumably willingness) to accept more risk is now substantially increased. Further, the income stream reduces the probability that Williams will need to borrow against plan assets to fund his children's college education. Thus, the Williams can accept a higher level of risk to achieve a higher total return in the plan.

The constraints on the portfolio are essentially unchanged. The time horizon for investments remains relatively long. A true investment time horizon might be 25 years, to coincide with the final payment from the trust, but three- to five-year checkpoint intervals would be advisable. The Williamses' already-low liquidity needs from their portfolio are now essentially negligible. Regulatory and legal constraints would be unchanged. The "unique circumstances" should now include the Williamses' greatly expanded wealth position and certainty of income flow. The $50,000, however, is a fixed sum, which will be eroded by inflation, so its purchasing power will be constantly diminishing through time.

Revised Asset Allocation

Williams should continue to emphasize growth-oriented investments in his personal account and total return in his profit-sharing account. Because the income stream from the trust is equivalent to a massive fixed-income investment, most of the bond fund should now be replaced with stocks. The long-term allocation to real estate also should increase to gain more diversification, inflation protection, and tax benefits.

Thus, the following allocation would be appropriate:

Profit-sharing assets:		
Common stock fund	$ 35,000	21%
Growth stock fund	70,000	40
Equity real estate	25,000	15
	$130,000	76%
Personal assets:		
Growth stock fund	$ 30,000	18%
Common stock (GTC)	10,000	6
	$ 40,000	24%
Combined assets:	$170,000	100%

The Williamses' portfolio, exclusive of their residential equity, now is more heavily weighted toward stocks (85 percent) plus 15 percent in equity real estate; no bonds are owned because the annuity takes their place, both for income and for diversification. Including the Williamses'equity in their residence, the unified mix would be 69 percent stocks, 31 percent equity real estate. The profit-sharing plan is now 81 percent equities, 19 percent real estate. The Williamses' personal account is now composed exclusively of the General Technology stock and the growth-stock mutual fund. The Williams should be encouraged to use their excess income to build an international stock fund holding in their personal account to gain the further diversification value of international exposure.

Industrial Products Corporation (A)

Industrial Products is a company contemplating a radical change—going private. To make the buyout viable, management wants to increase its pension portfolio returns in order to reduce the company's overall pension expense. The employees oppose any increase in risk to their retirement benefits. The task in this three-part case is to develop investment policies for both groups and to resolve the conflicts between the two.

Investment Policy Statement

An appropriate investment policy for the IPC pension fund, from management's perspective, will take the following considerations into account:

Objectives

Return Requirements: Focusing on FAS 87 pension expense reporting during the next five years, IPC management is interested in maximizing pension surplus, rather than increasing pension assets or decreasing contributions. To reduce costs and to improve the financial performance of the corporation, management expects to expand the pension surplus by achieving high portfolio returns. This return-maximization objective is compatible with management's high risk-tolerance level.

Risk Tolerance: IPC's management has indicated a willingness to have the pension fund adopt a high-risk posture, "aggressively seeking high portfolio returns" after the buyout. The pension plan is well funded currently, and management hopes to maximize the fund's contribution toward improving corporate finances before the company is taken public again. The relatively short horizon available to the fund and the requirements of ERISA are important considerations in determining the risk objective. On balance, the fund's risk capacity appears to be above average, subject to strict adherence to ERISA mandates.

Constraints

Liquidity: Unless the level of company contributions decreases dramatically, which is not expected, the pension fund has no unusual liquidity needs.

Time Horizon: Management has stated an objective of significantly improving IPC's financial performance during the next five years, after which it expects to take the company public again. Pragmatically, its time horizon for the pension fund is this five-year period. If its investment actions reflect a shorter and shorter horizon as the five-year period expires, however, conflict with ERISA's "exclusive benefit of the participants" rule is a possibility.

Laws and Regulations: As a qualified U.S. corporate retirement plan, management of the portfolio is subject to ERISA requirements, including the Prudent Expert standard.

Taxes: The IPC pension plan is tax-exempt.

Unique Preferences and Circumstances: Compared with a typical pension fund, IPC's fund has a relatively short time horizon, and management's current focus is on FAS 87 pension expense reporting. The presence of IBOs is also a nonstandard element that must be taken explicitly into account.

Industrial Products Corporation (B)

Investment Policy Statement

An appropriate investment policy for the IPC pension fund, from the employee (union) perspective, will embrace the following considerations:

Objectives

Return Requirements: Although the pension fund will be very sensitive to inflation because of built-in cost-of-living benefit increases for retirees, the employee perspective favors an income orientation. Returns should be of a type and progression that will support these inflation-linked benefits, so a total-return, capital-building orientation is preferable so long as income flows remain adequate to fund ongoing payments.

Risk Tolerance: The employees are primarily concerned with the security of their retirement benefits. They prefer a low-risk posture for the pension fund to the extent that it is consistent with producing a dependable, growing cash flow of adequate size.

Constraints

Liquidity: Nothing in the employee proposal appears to have changed the actual liquidity needs of the pension fund, but the union will probably expect the fund to retain a larger-than-normal reserve amount for contingencies and out of general conservatism.

Time Horizon: The employees' primary emphasis is on the security of the pension benefit in the context of a long-term horizon, probably well beyond 10 years. Any management attempt to invest the fund on a shorter and shorter term basis would be source of conflict.

Laws and Regulations: The union knows that IPC's pension plan is subject to the ERISA requirement that the fund be invested solely for the benefit of the plan participants. In negotiating a collective bargaining agreement, however, fiduciaries are free to fashion "whatever type of contract is agreeable to both parties." The employees will have a much more conservative interpretation of what is permissible than will management. This difference is another potential source of continuing friction between the two parties.

Taxes: The IPC pension plan is tax-exempt.

Unique Preferences and Circumstances: The employees have traded present compensation (lower salary growth and work force reduction) for higher future benefits (cost-of-living adjustment). Thus, they have made concessions and secured a greater degree of benefit security than is typical of corporate pension plans.

Industrial Products Corporation (C)

The employees' tolerance for risk must be viewed in the context of their desire to improve benefit security. Because FAS 87 applies, funding adequacy is measured by the plan surplus. The cost-of-living increases make the benefit liabilities quite sensitive to inflation. Whether Smith and the union recognize the asset-allocation implications of these facts is unclear.

The large bond holdings in the union's proposed asset allocation, in addition to being evidence of "conservatism," are actually deflation hedges. Because interest rates are positively correlated and bond prices are negatively correlated with inflation, the fund will depreciate just when it will be called upon to finance the cost-of-living increases. The revised asset allocation must call for much less of the total in bonds. Such a revision also better meets the higher return objective of management, because stocks should produce higher long-term returns than the fixed-income assets. The greater stability of bond returns is of no particular value in this case.

Historically, cash equivalents produce only small real rates of return over time. In the IPC context, cash equivalents do not meet management's objectives, nor do they serve employees' COLA benefit needs. Therefore, the fund should hold a minimum of cash equivalents for liquidity and safety purposes.

Real estate historically has been a good inflation hedge and has produced good real rates of return over the long term. A token allocation to real estate is present in the union's proposal, but a higher allocation to real estate is in order. It meets both employee and management objectives, especially the inflation-indexed benefits aspect of the retirement plan. Even after the company goes public again, a real estate component already in the portfolio should prove useful.

Equities have had mixed success as an inflation hedge in the short-term, but they have produced the best long-term returns of the asset classes available. Because the employees have a long-term time horizon and because real estate also can be used to enhance inflation protection, asset allocation should be revised to hold more stocks. Greater stock holdings would suit management's objectives as well.

The union proposal does not include a meaningful amount of non-U.S. equities, and international investments are not called for to meet any special pension fund need such as nondollar benefit payments. Even so, international investments are desirable for portfolio diversification and to increase return potential. An allocation to international securities of perhaps 15 percent appears in order. These holdings should lean more toward international equities than international bonds.

One acceptable asset allocation would be

	Range	Beginning
Domestic stocks	40-60%	50%
Domestic bonds	10-20	20
International stocks	5-10	10
Equity real estate	10-15	10
International bonds	5-10	5
Cash equivalents	0-5	5

This allocation meets management's objectives while providing reasonable protection of the employees' retirement benefits.

Universal Products, Inc.

This case provides an opportunity to consider whether an existing investment policy and asset allocation are still appropriate in the face of a revised economic forecast. The Assistant Treasurer of Universal Products, Inc. (UPI) has been asked to recommend appropriate revisions in the investment policies and asset allocations of the company's two retirement funds. He is also to present a case for or against use of equity real estate in the pension and profit-sharing portfolios.

Critique of Existing Investment Policy

The asset class restrictions now in place limit the two retirement plan portfolios to domestic stocks, domestic bonds, and cash equivalents. These restraints are inappropriate and counterproductive for at least the following reasons:

- The company has cut itself off from important opportunities to reduce investment risk and improve investment returns, which would benefit both itself and plan beneficiaries.
- If the Planning Committee is correct in its economic expectations (a sharp U.S. business downturn followed by extended stagflation), it should welcome the geographical diversification and accompanying favorable covariance from U.S. developments that investment in nondomestic securities would provide. In addition, it should be examining both international and real estate investment as possible inflation hedges and as means of enhancing returns.
- The restrictions are inconsistent with ERISA's emphasis on broad diversification for both types of retirement funds.

In addition to its overly narrow investment policy, UPI's Retirement Committee is either encouraging or permitting several other unsatisfactory conditions to prevail in the portfolios. These include

- No distinctions in investment content between the two portfolios in the face of a fundamental difference in where portfolio risk is borne;
- Inappropriate risk levels, arising from overemphasis on the equity asset class, and inadequate overall diversification;
- Within equities, inappropriate heavy emphasis on growth;
- Inadequate cash resources and inappropriate time horizons, especially for the profit-sharing portfolio;
- Inappropriate asset allocation in the profit-sharing portfolio relative to its purpose, funding, and risk-bearing circumstances; and
- Absence of individual decision making as to risk level or asset class exposures in the profit-sharing plan. (The company's decision applies to all participants, regardless of age, goals, circumstances, or preferences.)

Recommended Investment Policy

An appropriate investment policy for the retirement plans must consider the following factors:

Objectives

Return Requirements: Preservation of the existing capital base should be the primary return objective for both portfolios. This view is supported by the facts that (1) pension benefit payments may soon absorb all pension contributions, as well as pension portfolio income; (2) both portfolios have already gained from especially favorable investment results for the past several years; and (3) even moderately adverse economic conditions could be detrimental to this cyclical company's ability to service its pension obligations adequately and to continue to make profit-sharing contributions.

Risk Tolerance: Because of facts (1) and (3) above and because the company anticipates a downturn both in the economy and in its own fortunes, a below-average risk posture is indicated for both the pension and the profit-sharing portfolios. The profit-sharing plan has a lower capacity to bear risk than the pension plan because of a shorter average time horizon, the possible large need for liquidity in the short run, and the fact that the employees directly bear the risk of portfolio underperformance.

Constraints

Liquidity: If a recession does compel UPI to reduce its work force, the plans will need an above-average level of liquidity to provide for potential involuntary early retirements. The profit-sharing plan will be more vulnerable to withdrawals than will the pension plan.

Time Horizon: The plans have been operating in the context of a long-term investment horizon. This assumption may no longer be valid. UPI is a mature, cyclical company with an aging blue-collar work force, which may shrink in size in the relatively near term. The prospect of an imminent increase in payout argues for a shorter time horizon for both portfolios, but particularly for the profit-sharing portfolio.

Laws and Regulations: The plan is subject to ERISA provisions.

Taxes: The income the plans generate is either tax-exempt (pension or tax-deferred (profit sharing).

Unique Preferences and Circumstances: The company has an implied higher obligation of prudence for the profit-sharing portfolio than for the pension portfolio because the profit-sharing plan does not provide for individual allocation or asset class choices.

Critique of Existing Asset Allocation

Neither retirement portfolio is appropriately allocated at present. The portfolios should have a lower risk and better balance than is now in place. The profit-sharing portfolio should be even more conservatively oriented than the pension portfolio to reflect its possible extra liquidity needs, the absence of a company "deep pocket," and the uncertain risk-bearing abilities of the individual employees.

In the normal course of economic events, the extended "good times" of the past eight to nine years are likely to give way to at least a modest cyclical correction in the not-too-distant future, as the committee predicts. A downturn would have negative implications for equity market conditions and thus for the portfolios, with their heavy exposure in growth equities.

Given its relatively large size, the profit-sharing component of the retirement plan is of obvious importance to the workforce as a supplement to the defined-benefit pension component. Should the anticipated workforce shrinkage involve terminations and involuntary early retirements, in addition to scheduled retirements, the profit-sharing portfolio will experience a sudden need for extra liquidity as participants withdraw their vested ownership interests. At the same time, little or no excess income is expected from the pension portfolio. Therefore, present cash assets are not at an adequate level in either portfolio.

The present allocation of the profit-sharing portfolio is identical to that of the pension portfolio. This concurrence may be convenient for Jenson and the company, but it is not in the best interests of the participants because it ignores the significant differences between the two parties, particularly in risk-bearing capacity.

Recommended Asset Allocation

The company and the plan participants have been lucky in the past few years. Because the economy has had eight to nine good years, Jenson has been able to run growth-oriented portfolios, weighted heavily toward stocks. As a result, the investment performance of the portfolios has been especially favorable.

Credence must be given to the possibility of bad times developing within the planning horizon. Jenson's own expectations differ in degree but not in direction from the Planning Committee's. This threat suggests the need for hedging tactics with regard to the two retirement portfolios. They should reflect more conservatism and a more restrained approach to market exposure than they presently do.

In reallocating, attention must be given to how the profit-sharing and the pension components of the retirement plan differ in purpose and funding, in the incidence of risk bearing, and in time horizon. Under adverse economic conditions, profit-sharing plan withdrawals could swell, and company contributions could be displaced significantly or could even stop entirely. The profit-sharing plan's participants bear the risk of loss individually, even though the portfolio is invested collectively. The compositions of the two portfolios fail to reflect this distinction. Also, although the pension portfolio may warrant a long-term orientation, the horizon for any profit-sharing participant is only as long as the time until termination, involuntary early retirement, or scheduled retirement, whichever occurs first. At a time when the company is planning for deliberate shrinkage of the work force, this horizon may be quite short for a significant number of profit-sharing plan participants.

Pension Portfolio

To improve diversification, reduce risk, and enhance return potential under recession conditions, more of the pension portfolio should be in bonds, with laddered maturities. Stock exposure should be reduced and the remaining stock holdings broadened by reducing the growth-oriented component. Near-term economic uncertainty, fund maturity, and the need for more investment flexibility argue for establishment of a meaningful cash position. Close monitoring of the unfolding of actual events is essential and should guide future portfolio actions.

Given a continued ban on use of the international and real estate asset classes, an acceptable revised allocation of the pension portfolio would be as follows:

Cash equivalents	$ 11,000,000	10%
Domestic bonds	49,500,000	45
Domestic stocks	$ 49,500,000	45
	$110,000,000	100%

Profit-Sharing Portfolio

The same reasons that argue for a more conservative posture for the pension portfolio also apply to the profit-sharing portfolio. Additional circumstances apply specifically to the profit-sharing portfolio, however—shorter average time horizon, smaller capacity to bear risk, and possibly larger need for liquidity in the short run. Therefore, it should reflect even greater conservatism than the pension portfolio and move even further away from its present growth-oriented equity dominance.

An acceptable revised allocation would be

Cash equivalents	$11,000,000	20%
Domestic bonds	24,750,000	45
Domestic stocks	19,250,000	35
	$55,000,000	100%

Equity Real Estate

Although broadening the scope of permissible retirement portfolio investments to include equity real estate has much to recommend it, the benefits to be gained from actually investing in such assets depend on the specific characteristics of the plan.

Pension Portfolio

UPI's pension portfolio begs for improvement. It needs more diversification, a better risk-return profile, a higher cash-flow level, greater stability, and inflation protection. Equity real estate possesses attributes and characteristics that could prove helpful in each of these respects.

By improving diversification, both overall and within the equity group, and by providing low-to-negative covariance with most financial assets, the addition of equity real estate would be expected to raise long-term return prospects without increasing (and probably by decreasing) total portfolio risk. At the same time, the addition of such assets would directly address one of the Planning Committee's concerns by improving the inflation-hedge characteristics of the portfolio. An income-oriented equity real estate investment would tend to improve and stabilize the portfolio's income production and predictability, thereby addressing another area of concern.

At $110 million of total assets, the pension fund is large enough to take on an equity real estate exposure of meaningful size, even if the investment is un-marketable for some period of time in the future. Although the pension plan is maturing and its time horizon is no longer infinite, at least some portion of even a mature pension plan's total assets should continue to have a long-term orientation. Inclusion of an equity real estate component in this portion of UPI's pension investment total appears to be well within the bounds of prudence.

The conclusion is that the Retirement Committee should add equity real estate to the list of assets eligible for use in the pension portfolio. These new assets should be suitable income-oriented investments, initially to total $4 to $6 million. Eventually, this asset class should constitute about 10 percent of the portfolio.

Profit-Sharing Portfolio

Although the profit-sharing portfolio and the pension portfolio have similar shortcomings, the cure for these may be quite different because the two plans differ in a number of important respects. As compared to the pension plan, the profit-sharing plan has

- A shorter time horizon;
- Lower overall tolerance for risk;
- Risk bearing directly by participants;
- No company obligation to "make good" in the event of adverse overall investment experience;
- High potential liquidity demands from anticipated workforce shrinkage; and
- Capital preservation as the primary return objective (which is likely to be a particularly significant problem relatively soon).

On balance, the aggregate implication of these factors is that equity real estate is not suitable for this portfolio. A significant part of the improvement equity real estate might add to the profit-sharing portfolio is available from other sources. For example, the addition of nondollar bond and international equity components would importantly improve the portfolio's diversity and enhance its return-risk profile by introducing better covariance. Similarly, economic diversification should improve the stability of the cash-flow stream and provide at least some measure of inflation protection. The value of introducing an equity real estate component into the profit-sharing portfolio is marginal, given the horizon and liquidity considerations that must be taken into account.

A far better way for the company to change the way profit-sharing assets are allocated would be to allow participants individually to choose the assets that would best reflect their own particular goals, circumstances, and preferences. Their allocations would be tailored to them separately, not lumped together collectively. The company's responsibility would be to make available a variety of pooled or mutual fund investment vehicles, including a suitable equity real estate medium. Presumably, however, many of the participants already have some exposure to equity real estate in the form of the homes they own or are buying and would not choose to increase that exposure.

World Ecosystem Consortium (A)

This case introduces international considerations to the problem of setting investment policy for retirement funds. Because WEC has multicurrency benefit obligations, its investment policy must address currency risk in conjunction with the objectives and constraints of its retirement funds.

Investment Policy Statement

An appropriate investment policy statement for the WEC pension fund is:

Objectives

Return Requirements: Return objectives should emphasize total return, favoring capital growth over current income. With contributions and normal income widely exceeding payouts, the trust does not need to produce high levels of current income. Being tax-exempt, the trust is indifferent to income versus capital gains. The benefit obligations are multicurrency, so return objectives should be described in both dollar and nondollar terms, perhaps using an appropriately weighted currency index. Because a career-average benefit formula is used, the benefit obligations are not overly sensitive to inflation. Thus, real returns are somewhat less important than the production of nominal returns.

Risk Tolerance: Because the plan's benefit obligations are long term and the trust has no pressing liquidity or income needs, the portfolio can tolerate above-normal short-term volatility in investment returns. In addition, the pension trust is well funded, which enhances its capacity to bear risk. Because of these factors and because WEC intends to continue its conservative funding policy and to maintain the plan's "well-funded" status into the future, the net result is an above-average capacity to bear risk.

Constraints

Liquidity: Overall, the trust should experience a net inflow of cash for at least the next 10 years, automatically providing for any needed liquidity on an overall basis. Separately, a liquidity requirement in Canadian dollars does exist because of the large number of retirees in WEC's Canadian operations; this need must be specifically accommodated.

Time Horizon: The retirement plan is currently at an early stage of its life cycle, with net cash inflow and a high ratio of active to retired employees. Employees are generally young and many years from expected retirement. Therefore, the trust has a long-term time horizon extending well beyond 10 years. Again, the Canadian benefit obligation is an exception. The current large payments to retirees and the mature status of the Canadian operations indicate a shorter time horizon for these obligations.

Laws and Regulations: The trust must comply with ERISA provisions.

Taxes: The plan is a qualified, tax-exempt retirement plan. The trust may be subject to nonresident withholding taxes on some international investments.

Unique Preferences and Circumstances: The trust has two unique features. First, the benefit obligations are multicurrency; investment returns and currency risk must be viewed in that perspective. Second, the Canadian benefit obligations are significantly different from the other benefit obligations in their liquidity requirements and time horizon. Investment actions must address these special needs.

Asset Allocation

Based on the investment policy, an appropriate asset allocation should address the following specifics: above-average risk-taking capability; production of high nominal total returns in multicurrencies; a moderate inflation protection requirement; a liquidity need only for Canadian dollars; and a long-term time horizon, except in Canada. These specifics indicate an asset allocation that is multicurrency and equity dominated, with broad asset-class exposure.

Both domestic and international equities have higher expected returns than bonds and can help the trust meet its objective of high nominal total returns. The higher risk in equities is within the trust's risk-taking capability and long-term time horizon.

A majority of the equities in the asset allocation should be international stocks. Hedging the currency exposure is generally unnecessary because the benefit obligations are multicurrency in nature. The international investments should be diversified over the major world securities markets, especially those in countries where the plan has benefit obligations.

As with equities, a majority of the bonds should be international bonds. Bonds can provide important diversification and risk-reduction benefits in the trust and would also help meet the fixed-benefit obligations to current retirees. The special circumstances in Canada indicate a need for larger holdings of both short- and long-term Canadian obligations, tailored to the actual retired-lives pattern there.

Although stocks are generally viewed as an inflationary hedge, past history shows that they may not perform well in periods of high or rising inflation. A significant position in equity real estate should be included for its ability to produce good inflation-adjusted returns.

Only in Canada are cash equivalents necessary for liquidity. There, of course, Canadian dollar holdings are appropriate. Given the investment policy, the portfolio should be invested according to the following guidelines: 50 to 70 percent in equities, 20 to 30 percent in bonds, 5 to 10 percent in real estate, and up to 5 percent in cash equivalents.

One appropriate asset allocation would be

International stocks	35%
Domestic stocks	25
International bonds	15
Domestic bonds	10
Real estate	10
Canadian cash equivalents	5
	100%

Summarized by asset class, the allocation is

Equities, including real estate	70%
Fixed-income, excluding cash	25
Canadian cash equivalents	5
	100%

Or, summarized by market representation, the asset allocation is

International securities	50%
Domestic securities	35
Real estate	10
Canadian cash equivalents	5
	100%

World Ecosystem Consortium (B)

The Committee's proposed benefit formula changes would require immediate recalculation of the projected benefit obligation (PBO). An employee retiring after the benefit formula change would have his or her pension calculated on the basis of final-year salary, which is almost certainly higher than the career-average salary. Thus, changing the benefit formula from career-average salary to final-year salary would increase the accrued and projected benefit obligations of the pension plan. In addition, any ad hoc pension increase for current retirees would also increase the accrued benefit obligation (ABO). The plan would immediately become less "well-funded," and the trust would have less capacity to bear risk, even though the time horizon would not change.

Because the benefit obligation would increase, the company's pension expense and its contributions into the trust would also increase. Current pension payments would also rise, depending on the amount of any ad hoc pension augmentation for current retirees. Taken together, the net cash inflow into the trust may be unchanged, although additional information is needed to make an exact determination. The benefit formula change should initially have little impact on the liquidity needs of the trust.

The proposed change would make the benefit obligation more sensitive to inflation, which is the Committee's intention. The effect of wage inflation on the final salary is direct, whereas its effect on career-average salary is diluted by the averaging process. The ad hoc inflation adjustments for retirees also increase the benefit obligation in inflationary periods. The "unwritten policy" dictum avoids contractual obligation and hence does not affect the FAS 87 calculation of the projected benefit obligation. Nevertheless, its effect is real and should be recognized in the investment policy. The term "high levels" with respect to inflation rates as the trigger for ad hoc benefit increases is vague, and it should be defined better in order to reduce uncertainty in planning for investment implementation.

The revised asset allocation should reflect a reduced risk profile and provide better inflation protection. The asset allocation revision should reduce stocks and increase bonds for risk reduction. Real estate should be increased for additional inflation protection. Cash equivalents may also be considered an inflation hedge, because short-term interest rates typically adjust to inflation eventually. Cash equivalents involve a large total-return sacrifice, however, because of their lower expected long-term returns.

One appropriate revised asset allocation would be

		Change
International stocks	25%	−10%
Domestic stocks	20	−5
International bonds	20	+5
Domestic bonds	15	+5
Real estate	15	+5
Canadian cash equivalents	5	0
	100%	

Summarized by asset class, the allocation is

Equities, including real estate	60%	−10%
Fixed-income, excluding cash	35	+10
Canadian cash equivalents	5	0
	100%	

Or, summarized by market representation, the allocation is

International stocks	45%	−5%
Domestic stocks	35	0
Real estate	15	+5
Canadian cash equivalents	5	+0
	100%	

Good Samaritan Hospital (A)

Because Mrs. Atkins is now expected to live no more than nine months, investment policy for her portfolio should begin to look beyond the current circumstances to the likely creation of the Atkins Endowment Fund. The first part of this case illustrates the unique investment considerations of endowment funds in contrast with those appropriate for a wealthy individual investor. The second part deals with the fundamentals of investing for endowments. The third part provides an opportunity to modify an investment strategy for different economic and capital market expectations.

Investment Policy

Investment policy for Mrs. Atkins portfolio must express her investment objectives and consider all relevant constraints on the achievement of the portfolio. The return requirements, risk tolerance, time horizon, and legal and regulatory considerations will not change significantly.

Objectives

Return Requirements: Mrs. Atkins requires a minimum of $50,000 after-tax investment income annually. Future investment income growth should attempt to keep pace with inflation. Given the fact that the assets will go to a charitable remainderman at Mrs. Atkins' death, capital growth is also needed. The hospital is currently targeting a 6 percent income return, which is consistent with Mrs. Atkins' own income objective.

Risk Tolerance: Mrs. Atkins can afford to take moderate risk to achieve income growth with some capital appreciation, given that her $50,000 minimum income need, adjusted for future inflation, is met. If the fund becomes large enough, somewhat increased risk could be incurred to facilitate growth of capital.

Constraints

Liquidity: The liquidity constraint should perhaps be changed from "low" to "moderate" to reflect greater uncertainty during the next year. Mrs. Atkins may have heavy medical expenses; furthermore, she may live longer than is currently expected but remain in poor health. Also, after her death, the presence of cash reserves may facilitate reinvestment for the endowment's purposes. Thus, somewhat greater consideration could be given to liquidity.

Time Horizon: Mrs. Atkins' shorter-than-average time horizon is not an important investment consideration because her wealth will go to an endowment fund, which has an infinite time horizon, on her death.

Laws and Regulations: Endowment funds are subject to state regulatory and legal constraints, and Prudent Man standards generally apply. These constraints do not conflict with prudent investment of Mrs. Atkins' portfolio while she is alive.

Taxes: The most important area of change concerns taxes. Mrs. Atkins is in the maximum tax bracket for income and capital gains, whereas the endowment fund operates free of taxes. Therefore, tax policy for the portfolio should emphasize favorable tax benefits in the short term and postpone actions having unfavorable tax consequences. The analyst should seek agreement on taking capital losses to offset the $50,000 gain already realized on earlier sales of the Merit stock and on deferring further capital gains until the tax-exempt endowment fund receives the assets. Sales to take losses would also create the cash that would increase liquidity.

Unique Preferences and Circumstances: The investment of the Atkins portfolio must reflect the objectives and constraints of the Good Samaritan Hospital—the beneficiary of the assets upon Mrs. Atkins' death—when they do not conflict with those of Mrs. Atkins. The major constraint for her is the tax consequences.

Asset Allocation

The policy statement concerning asset allocation does not require immediate change in asset allocation ranges but should no longer specify that fixed-income and short-term investments be "principally tax-exempt."

Specific Investment Actions

Several specific investment actions should be taken with regard to the Atkins portfolio. Mrs. Atkins should agree to sell her Caterpillar Tractor and Weyerhauser stocks, as well as the three municipal bonds that are selling significantly below cost. The capital losses generated from these sales would more than offset the $50,000 gain in Merit stock already taken this year. (The Deere convertible bonds have a slight loss, but the transaction costs would outweigh the small loss realized.) A desirable action to preserve the pre-existing asset proportions would be to reinvest the common stock proceeds into new common stock holdings and the bond proceeds into new bonds, depending on capital market expectations. A modest increase in short-term reserves is indicated for a portion of the fixed-income money. Such reserves should be kept in tax-exempt issues, but longer maturities could be put into taxable bonds, because these can later be held in the endowment fund, which is not subject to federal taxation; their presence would have only minor adverse tax consequences for Mrs. Atkins in the short run.

Good Samaritan Hospital (B)

With the death of Mrs. Atkins, the hospital now owns the Atkins trust assets. The task here is to reallocate the trust portfolio to the hospital's greatest benefit.

Because income from the hospital's existing endowment assets has proved adequate to meet its current operating deficit, the new assets provided by the Atkins Endowment Fund should be invested primarily to provide future growth in income. Historic data show that equities provide superior long-term total return. In addition, with the current portfolio endowment producing a 6 percent yield, sufficient to cover the operating deficit, an equity ratio below 60 percent would generate current income in excess of the stated objective of the Board of Governors. An equity range of 60 to 80 percent is preferred.

An endowment fund's long time horizon and limited liquidity needs would also permit assumption of the risk associated with the higher level of equities. The hospital's operating expenses will surely continue to rise with inflation, so the Atkins Endowment Fund should contain the highest equity representation (stocks, real estate, and the like) consistent with the hospital's income needs and other constraints.

Investment Policy Statement

Given that Good Samaritan's existing endowment assets are adequate to cover expected average operating deficits, and in the absence of other known requirements, the following set of objectives and constraints appears appropriate for the Atkins Endowment Fund:

Objectives

Return Requirements: Although the fund should strive to provide a predictable stream of income growing in line with inflation, the primary return goal is growth of principal over time. These incremental assets represent a key element of Good Samaritan's long-term viability; their important return contribution will be in total return, not in current income.

Risk Tolerance: In view of the endowment's long time horizon, limited liquidity needs, and the adequacy of income on the already-existing endowment assets to offset the operating deficit, the incremental Atkins Fund element can assume an above-average level of risk.

Constraints

Liquidity: Liquidity needs are low. Except for investment purposes and periodic payment of accumulated income, the fund requires no sizable liquid reserve.

Time Horizon: Endowment funds typically have very long time horizons, and apparently the current case is no exception. Certainly, Good Samaritan's time horizon extends well beyond a normal market cycle.

Laws and Regulations: Most endowment funds are governed by state regulations, which embrace a Prudent Man standard. Other regulatory and legal constraints should not be significant investment factors here.

Taxes: Because the endowment funds of charitable organizations are normally tax-exempt, tax considerations are not a meaningful constraint for this fund.

Unique Preferences and Circumstances: Although the details provided concerning Good Samaritan are somewhat sketchy, and additional information might be appropriately requested, this hospital appears to be experiencing the financial difficulties that have characterized the industry for several years. The existence of an operating deficit, and the possibility that this deficit may grow, suggest that a slightly more conservative posture relative to other endowment funds might be appropriate. The 6 percent income demand will itself result in such a posture.

Portfolio Revisions: Transition

The portfolio should immediately eliminate all tax-exempt securities and replace them with taxable securities that will provide a higher level of after-tax income. Notwithstanding its request that no major new sale or purchase programs be undertaken, the Board will probably agree to such action. To guard against a decline in interest rates before the new investment policy is established, the municipal bond proceeds should be reinvested primarily in a portfolio of government bonds of approximately the same duration as the existing municipal portfolio. The use of government bonds would provide the most liquidity and minimum transaction costs in case other instruments are ultimately deemed more appropriate.

Because sales of Merit stock will no longer give rise to a tax liability and because the Board is unlikely to have any personal attachment to Merit, the Board should sell one-fourth to one-third of the Merit Enterprises stock to provide funds for diversification purposes.

Specific Actions

The hospital's economic and capital market expectations are quite favorable. No recession is forecast, and inflation is expected to remain moderate. Very substantial positive returns for both stocks and bonds are forecast, suggesting that short-term reserves should be minimal.

Bond-return expectations are rather close to those for common stocks, yet bonds provide lower risk as measured by the standard deviation. Therefore, within the 20-percentage-point range of variation (60 to 80 percent for stocks, 20 to 40 percent for bonds) bonds should be used more heavily than stocks. Thus, 65 percent of the account could be invested in common stocks and 35 percent in bonds, with no short-term reserves beyond those needed for minimal liquidity requirements.

Taxable bonds should immediately replace the municipal bonds. Because these bonds currently represent 35 percent of the portfolio, no net increase or decrease in the aggregate market value of bond holdings would result.

The proceeds of Merit sales and the existing short-term reserves should be used to add additional issues to the common stock portfolio and to increase modestly the holdings of existing issues. A reasonable ultimate objective would be to have approximately 20 issues in the $1.3 million (65 percent) equity portfolio, suggesting an average position size of perhaps $65,000.

Good Samaritan Hospital (C)

Investment Associates' economic and capital market forecasts differ from those the Good Samaritan Board provided.

Given the dimension of the changes the Board's forecasts imply, the bond allocation should be reduced to 20 percent, which is the minimum implied by the 60 percent to 80 percent equity allocation range. The equity target should be at the low end as well, perhaps at 60 percent, because the return expectations are now somewhat lower. The inflation-hedging qualities of common stock and real estate investments, however, suggest that they should continue to represent a major portion of the portfolio over the longer term. The remaining 20 percent of total assets would be kept in Treasury bills as a buying reserve.

As before, taxable bonds should replace the municipal bonds. In view of the reduced, 20 percent target for bonds, however, only $400,000 in taxable bonds should be purchased. In addition, the duration of the bond portfolio should be substantially shortened. Although the standard deviation of return expectations is much lower now (suggesting less risk or more confidence), the return expectations themselves no longer justify the risk of owning longer bonds.

The sale of Merit Enterprises to provide greater diversification is still recommended. In fact, this diversification effort might be intensified. The proceeds of such sales should be used to begin the development of an equity real estate portfolio (eventually to constitute 10 to 15 percent of the total portfolio) and to purchase international stocks to improve diversification and total return potential.

Appendix

Appendix Table A

Rates of Return and Standard Deviations
for Various Types of Assets

Asset Class	Compound Annual Rates of Return				Volatility	
	5 Years 1985-89	10 Years 1980-89	20 Years 1970-89	30 Years 1960-89	Standard Deviation	Period Covered
Domestic equities						
Common stocks*	20.40	17.55	11.55	10.29	15.89	1960-89
Small-company stocks*	10.34	15.83	13.64	14.26	26.72	1960-89
Growth funds**	17.78	15.19	9.69	10.17	17.55	1960-89
Income funds**	15.54	15.34	11.61	10.08	11.27	1960-89
*International equities (U.S. returns)**						
World equity markets	24.83	15.78	9.07	N/A	16.46	1969-89
EAFE Index	34.17	19.55	12.46	N/A	22.50	1969-89
Corporate bonds	15.02	13.03	9.58	6.88	11.29	1960-89
*Government obligations**						
Long-term bonds	15.49	12.60	9.00	6.42	11.06	1960-89
Intermediate-term bonds	11.37	11.91	9.42	7.40	6.54	1960-89
Treasury bills	6.81	8.89	7.59	6.34	2.90	1960-89
*Municipal bonds**	7.66	9.10	7.54	6.37	2.44	1960-89
Real Estate						
Commercial property index***	8.11	11.06	N/A	N/A	4.91	1978-89
New single-family houses**	2.16	4.00	6.65	N/A	3.98	1963-89
Real estate investment trusts**	−6.47	2.24	N/A	N/A	27.87	1971-89
*Commodities**						
Commodity spot market	0.26	−0.98	4.18	3.31	13.77	1960-89
Crude oil spot prices	−10.27	−5.94	13.68	7.87	59.07	1960-89
*Precious metals**						
Gold	5.30	−2.57	12.92	8.49	31.75	1960-89
Silver	−4.22	−13.58	5.41	5.95	52.98	1960-89
Economic indicators						
Real GNP	3.33	2.60	2.70	3.14		
Inflation (CPI)	3.67	5.10	6.22	4.97		
Prime rate	9.35	11.64	10.14	8.58		

Sources:
* Roger G. Ibbotson, and Rex A. Sinquefield, *Stocks, Bonds, Bills, and Inflation* (SBBI), 1982, updated in *Stocks, Bonds, Bills, and Inflation 1990 Yearbook*, Ibbotson Associates, Chicago. All rights reserved.
** C. David Chase, *Chase Investment Performance Digest*, 1990 edition, Chase Global Data & Research, Inc. 289 Great Road, Acton, MA 01720. All rights reserved.
*** Based on the Frank Russell Commercial Real Estate Quarterly Property Index.

Appendix Table B

Correlations of Asset Class Total Returns, 1971-87

	Stocks	Long-Term Govt. Bonds	Intermediate Govt. Bonds	Treasury Bills	Real Estate	Small Stocks	Foreign Stocks	Foreign Bonds	Inflation
Stocks	1.00								
Long-Term Government Bonds	0.37	1.00							
Intermediate Government Bonds	0.36	0.96	1.00						
Treasury Bills	-0.06	-0.02	0.23	1.00					
Real Estate	0.13	-0.31	-0.19	0.58	1.00				
Small Stocks	0.74	0.12	0.14	0.07	0.33	1.00			
Foreign Stocks	0.66	0.21	0.07	-0.40	-0.09	0.32	1.00		
Foreign Bonds	0.20	0.48	0.28	-0.54	-0.41	0.05	0.64	1.00	
Inflation	-0.32	-0.59	-0.51	0.45	0.50	0.05	-0.51	-0.54	1.00

Note: The period 1971-87 is the longest for which annual return data are available for all of the asset classes.

Source: Roger Ibbotson and Larry Siegel, "How to Forecast Long-Run Asset Returns," *Investment Management Review* (now *Investing* magazine), September/October, 1988, pp. 30-39.